**East Africa:
In Search of National
and Regional Renewal**

EAST AFRICA
In Search of National
and Regional Renewal

Edited by

Felicia Arudo Yieke

COUNCIL FOR THE DEVELOPMENT OF
SOCIAL SCIENCE RESEARCH IN AFRICA

ISBN: 2-86978-144-X
Page layout: Hadijatou Sané
Cover Design: Ibrahima Fofana
Impression: Lightning Source

CODESRIA would like to express its gratitude to African Governments, the Swedish
Development Co-operation Agency (SIDA/SAREC), the International Development
Research Centre (IDRC), OXFAM GB/I, the MacArthur Foundation, the Carnegie
Corporation, the Norwegian Ministry of Foreign Affairs, the Danish Agency for
International Development (DANIDA), the French Ministry of Cooperation, the
Ford Foundation, the United Nations Development Programme (UNDP), the
Rockefeller Foundation, the Prince Claus Fund and the Government of Senegal for
support of its research, publication and training activities.

Contents

Notes on Contributors

Maurice N. Amutabi received his undergraduate and graduate education at the University of Nairobi in Kenya. He is currently a Fulbright fellow in the department of History, University of Illinois at Urbana-Champaign, USA. He is well published, and his books and articles include the following among many others; *Nationalism and Democracy for People-centred Development in Africa* [2000] (with E.M. Were), and *Islam and Underdevelopment in Africa* (forthcoming).

Chachage S.L. Chachage is currently Professor and head of department of Sociology at the University of Dar es Salaam, where he has served as Associate Dean (Research and Publications). Professor Chachage has also taught at the University of Cape Town, held many positions of distinction and served on the editorial boards of several journals. He has published extensively on Sociology, and is a well renowned Swahili language novelist.

Mohammed Kulumba is the co-ordinator of undergraduate programmes in the department of Political Science and Public Administration at Makerere University in Uganda. He is also a lecturer in the same department. He is currently pursuing his PhD at Makerere University. He has published on a wide range of topics, which include among others; public policy and management, religion and conflict, interest groups and civil society, state external intervention, HIV and AIDS, comparative politics, and gender and decentralised government.

Sangai Mohochi holds an MA in Kiswahili studies from Egerton University in Kenya. He is a Kiswahili lecturer at Egerton University although he is currently on a two-year Swahili teaching fellowship at St Lawrence University in Canton, USA. At the same time, he is a registered PhD student under sponsorship of DAAD (German Academic Exchange Programme). He has published seven journal articles to date, while several others are at different stages of the publishing process.

Emmanuel Okoth Manyasa is a tutorial fellow at Kenyatta University in Kenya in the department of Economics. He teaches developmental Economics and statistics, and also has interests in ethnicity and rural development. He is also a director of the centre for ethnic mainstreaming. He is a registered PhD student at Kenyatta University and is currently working on a number of publications.

Issa Shivji was the first Tanzanian professor of Law. He works at University of Dar es Salaam, and is also a practising advocate. He is the recipient of Honorary Doctor of Law from the University of East London, and was also awarded the Faculty of Law silver Jubilee Awards for the most prolific Tanzanian Academician, and the University of Dar es Salaam 'scholar of the Millennium' Award, 2002. He has published over fifteen books and monographs and some seventy articles in scholarly journals.

Felicia Yieke has a PhD in Applied Linguistics from University of Vienna, Austria. She did her undergraduate studies and Masters degree studies at Kenyatta University (Kenya) and Moi University (Kenya) respectively. She currently teaches at Egerton University in the department of Languages and Linguistics. Her research interests include Discourse Analysis, Corporate communication, Sociolinguistics, especially in the area of Gender Analysis and Language. She has published considerably in refereed International journals.

Bahru Zewde is Emeritus Professor of History at Addis Ababa University, Chairman of the Board of the Forum for Social Studies, Resident Vice-President of the Organization for Social Science Research in Eastern and Southern Africa and currently Editor of CODESRIA's *Africa Review of Books.*

Introduction

Felicia A. Yieke

The Council for the Development of Social Science Research in Africa (CODESRIA) celebrated its 30th anniversary in 2003. Established in 1973, through the collective will of African social science researchers, the Council was created to be a forum through which scholars could transcend barriers to knowledge production and, in so doing, play a critical role in the democratic development of the continent.

As part of the series of events planned to mark the anniversary, five sub-regional conferences were organised in Central, East, North, Southern and West Africa. These sub-regional conferences were followed by a grand finale conference held at the Council's headquarters in Dakar, Senegal, in December 2003. The papers in this volume are part of a selection, and were first presented at the Eastern Africa sub-regional conference, which convened in Addis Ababa, Ethiopia, on 30 and 31 October 2003, under the theme of East Africa: In Search of National and Regional Renewal.

The East African sub-region presents an interesting mix of experiences which, both historically and contemporaneously, have been at the heart of some of the main preoccupations of African nationalists and of the quest for the realisation of the pan-African ideal. Identified by Archaeological Research as the place of origin of humankind, the sub-region is significant in African history in several other important respects. It is home to the only African country – Ethiopia – that escaped direct colonial rule and whose resistance to Italian military invasion was instrumental in galvanising African resistance to foreign domination. Precisely for this reason, Addis Ababa was readily designated the Headquarters of the Organisation of African Unity (OAU), when it was established and as a consequence, the sub-region has played host to some of the most important moments in the post-independence African quest for collective action. Furthermore, several of the giants of African nationalism, as well as some of the boldest experiments seeking to give content to independence, were undertaken in East Africa. In this connection, the personal example of Mwalimu Julius Nyerere and the attempts he made to concretise the ideals of African nationalism are perhaps the most consistent and outstanding. He promoted the Africanisation of governance structures, the adoption of Swahili as the official language of Tanzania, the ideals of self-reliance, and the investment of energies in the building of the East African Community. He offered unwavering support to the liberation struggles in Southern Africa, and also launched the Ujamaa programme. The experiment in African socialism, which Nyerere embraced, was not the only path regional leaders pursued. Tanzania's immediate neighbour, Kenya, which was led by Jomo Kenyatta, who was another giant of African nationalism and veteran of the pre-independence resistance to British rule opted for a completely different approach, which consisted essentially in the adoption of a private capitalist system of development with a strong accent on foreign investment. Ethiopia itself was governed for a long time by a hereditary monarchy until Haile Selassie's rule was brought to an end through a military takeover. The monarchy was abolished and the country was subsequently proclaimed a Marxist state. In sum, the countries of the sub-region have experienced regime types that spanned the ideological spectrum, and in some cases such as Siad Barre's Somalia, involved official swings from one ideological framework to another in line with the exigencies of political survival and shifting Cold War alliances.

Whether colonised or not, and irrespective of the ideological and policy choices they made, all of the countries of East Africa faced numerous and broadly similar challenges of nation-building and socio-economic development. These problems were not eased by the various burdens of history that played an important part in shaping domestic political alliances in contexts which are highly pluralistic, especially along ethnic and religious lines, and which exhibited significant levels of social polarisation. As a consequence, the sub-region was exposed to major conflicts both of an inter-state and intra-state nature that implicated virtually all the countries in the area. The worst of these conflicts have been played out in Uganda, Ethiopia, Eritrea, Sudan, Somalia, Djibouti, the Zanzibar component of Tanzania, and the Comoros. While the roots of the conflicts are varied and open to debate, their consequences have been similar: a reinforcement of political authoritarianism, a widening of the gulf between state and society, an exacerbation of social inequalities and a widespread disruption of economic activities. Prolonged conflict has also weakened the state apparatus, even as several of the countries succumbed to military rule. In all cases, de facto and de jure single party rule was imposed in one form or the other at some point after the achievement of independence. It was only in the period from the 1980s onwards, that concerted pressure, mainly from social movements, began to push most of the regimes in power towards a reform of the political space. As in the rest of Africa, much of the reform effort entailed the adoption or re-introduction of multiparty politics, a significant exception being Uganda under Yoweri Museveni and the so-called 'movement system' on the basis of which the NRM has exercised power. Political decentralisation exercises and efforts at constitutional reform have also been undertaken, including the ethno-regionalist federalist model introduced in Ethiopia after the fall of the Marxist-inclined Dergue. Furthermore, there has been a revival of interest in the sub-region in the rebirth of co-operation and integration processes aimed at promoting common inter-state objectives and seeking shared solutions.

An overview of the challenges facing East Africa would suggest that in the main, these centre around the accommodation and management of diversity; the re-thinking of citizenship in the framework of a renewed social contract between state and society; the expansion of the base for social inclusion, especially concerning the rural and urban working poor; the promotion of a civic culture underpinned by basic democratic rights, which pays particular attention to disaffected youth; the revitalisation of associational life in a direction that strengthens popular democratic participation; the restoration of a developmental agenda to the policy process; the promotion of an all-round project of regionalisation; the encouragement of the further opening up of the political space to allow for greater accountability; and the rebuilding of the state and the policy process in an environment of peace and stability. These challenges lie at the heart of the quest for national and sub-regional renewal. The extent to which they are achieved will also be crucial to the realisation of the ideals of autonomous development and social justice that, in the first place, fired African Nationalism and the Pan-African movement.

The papers in this volume therefore explore different dimensions of the challenges confronting the countries of the East African region. Issa Shivji looks at the rise of post-war Nationalism in Africa and its true essence. For him, the quintessence of Nationalism was, and still is anti-imperialism. It was thus a demand and struggle against, rather than for something: an expression of a people as an antidote to white supremacist rule. The 'National Question' in Africa (which reflects all the struggles in Africa and most of the third world countries), whose expression is nationalism thus remains unresolved so long as there is imperialist domination. However, whatever the scope, Shivji echoes what Nyerere himself was to admit: that African Nationalism is incomplete without Pan-Africanism. It would in fact be meaningless, anachronistic and dangerous.

Shivji then goes on to look at the debunking of Nationalism in the post-cold war period under the apparent hegemony of neo-liberalism and the so-called globalisation (how Nationalism is being annihilated by the assault of imperialism in the new garb of Globalisation). In this phase, the Pan-African ideal does not find even a lip service among the new proponents of the 'African Renaissance'. The African Renaissance is thus seen as worse than a pale copy of Kwame Nkrumah's African personality, and thus utterly uninspiring. Shivji decries the fact that in most of the African states, the foreign policy has moved from the one based on 'African freedom and African unity' to that based on 'economic diplomacy'. The Neo-liberal discourse and political rhetoric has therefore been to debunk Nationalism on the one hand, and rehabilitate imperialism on the other. At the same time, intellectually, the majority of African intellectuals have been pretty well accommodated in the mainstream.

Shivji eventually makes an effort to explore how the 'National Question' can be re-articulated and re-configured with the democratic and social questions to make it more relevant to Africa. He argues for a new Nationalism to counter Imperialism in its globalisation phase, to resolve the National Question and hopefully pave the way for social emancipation; he anticipates an insurrection of a second Nationalism.

Chachage Seithy Chachage in his interrogation of the intellectual community, talks about the new partnership for Africa's development (NEPAD) as an intellectual product of some of the African intellectuals. His choice of NEPAD is a deliberate one since in this programme, one finds a confluence of lack of creativity and lack of collective memory among many African leaders and intellectuals. This, he says is ironic since NEPAD makes claims of the renewal and regeneration of Africa within attempts to unite it (Africa). Chachage acknowledges that in recent years, we have had many fundamental critiques of NEPAD from all over the continent. He notes that it is to these intellectuals who are concerned with the possibilities of transcending neo-liberalism that we as Africans must turn to, if we have to grasp the actual role of intellectuals in that search for renewal in Africa.

He decries the fact that the world today has reached a situation whereby the state no longer needed the services of the intellectuals for purposes of legitimation as it was once the case in history. Many of the educated in Africa have thus become willing accomplices of the forces that worked against the emancipation of the people of Africa, hardly producing any solutions in thinking as far as the problems facing Africa are concerned (they have their priorities misplaced). At the same time, many intellectuals were increasingly becoming ignorant of what is or was happening to their neighbouring countries due to lack of regional, continental and even Pan-Africanist historicity. Chachage sees colonialism, neo-colonialism and imperialism as re-packaged under Globalisation, and says that it is a pity that in Africa today, there are intellectuals who still believe in the mythologies of globalisation: which is a process that amounts to no more than an intellectual programme of desired goals. He terms these intellectuals as socially irresponsible individuals who are perpetuating abuse, prejudices, mediocrity, regressive and repressive interests wrapped in forms of 'universalism of the west', which is essentially false.

Chachage concludes that if we are to seriously take the clarion call for an African Renaissance or Renewal, then the pre-condition for that is the existence of a body of critical intellectuals, who are first and foremost capable of taking the immense responsibility of being competent, besides being a moral authority who is fully committed to the politics of the radical witnesses. This is a community of intellectuals who are ready and capable of defending the ideals of social justice.

Sangai Mohochi looks at the establishment of the African Union in place of the moribund Organisation of African Unity (OAU) as a way of enhancing regional integration. He sees language in such a situation as an effective communication tool to bring people of diverse origins together, and to work towards a common goal. His argument is that the development of African languages, and NOT foreign languages would be a necessary tool in fostering the African Union, and making it a reality. The African language for him is that language, which is easily accessible to the majority. He notes that by insisting on English and other foreign languages as we in Africa are doing now, we are only succeeding in shutting out about 80 per cent of our population from active and popular participation in the development process. He quotes Igue and Noueni (1994), who assert that development can never occur when the great majority are marginalised by the use of a language, which simply allows an elite to conduct a monologue with itself. For him, our continued reliance on foreign languages is one way of perpetuating the Neo-colonialism that our Pan-Africanist leaders consistently and persistently spoke out against.

Mohochi adds that while making decisions on language matters, we probably need to be driven by an assessment of the language use demands in Africa against the available language resource, since Africa is multilingual. He floats Swahili as a forerunner for the position of an African lingua franca, and he gives us a list of scholars who have also advocated for this choice. These scholars see Swahili as the only linguistic export from Africa that has gained wide currency, acceptance and recognition, and even suggest that such a language should be able to meet the communication needs of various international organisations as a possible world language.

In the face of all the many languages that Africa would have to pick for the African Union, Mohochi ultimately proposes functional multilingualism as a possible compromise between the preservation of our traditions and modernisation. He suggests a development of local languages since everyone has linguistic human rights to enjoy in life; regional languages for wider communication beyond our communities; Swahili for long-term communication in the African Union; and other foreign languages for international interaction. Mohochi thus advocates for a shift in language policy in the region, if the quest for regional integration is to become a reality.

Felicia Yieke, in her paper, also looks at the language question but in the East African Parliament. She says that although the East African Community was formed after the countries within the region got independence, it was disbanded by 1977. However, there was later renewed interest in the search of national and regional integration within the East African region, and this occasioned the revival of the East African community. Additionally, there was the creation of the East African Parliament that was supposed to chart the way forward for the countries in the region, in terms of social, economic and political improvements of the states involved. The questions Yieke asks are as follows: Which language will be adopted as the working language for the parliament? Which language will maintain the national identities of the regions and yet re-invent regionalism, while at the same time ensuring that there is linguistic gender sensitivity within the parliament?

Yieke highlights reasons why the language question is pertinent in parliament. She gives various guidelines for points of consideration in the process of choosing a language that will serve all nations in an integrative manner without taking away from the people their various national identities. She hopes that this paper will eventually give the readers a clear linguistic positioning of a renewed East African reality, and its implications for the further strengthening of the community, and the East African parliament in particular.

Emmanuel Okoth Manyasa examines the issue of ethnicity in Africa, and highlights the various threats it poses to the process of development. He sees an identity dilemma in Africa today, where ethnic and national loyalties are in competition and conflict. Ethnic sub-nationalism has replaced Nationalism and Pan-Africanism that powered the struggle for independence. In this case, plurality and diversity, which ideally are expected to provide a positive pool of resources, have now become a burden on the continent, and everything is increasingly being viewed and appreciated through ethnic lenses. Manyasa addresses the issues of ethnicism and ethnocentricism as factors in the political stability, good governance and economic mobilisation in Africa. He gives as examples the successive periods of turmoil in Uganda between 1962 and 1986, the tribal clashes that rocked Kenya in the 1990s, the ethnic conflicts between the Amhara and Eritreans in Ethiopia, the situation in Somalia, the Sudan, Mozambique, Angola and the Democratic Republic of Congo, just to mention a few.

There is a lot of pretence amongst the African nations as far as ethnicity is concerned, and this is detrimental to the sustainability of most African states. Manyasa sees liberal democracy (an import from the west) as not having improved ethnic relations in most countries. On the contrary, it has served to heighten competitive ethnic consciousness, ethnicise political competition, increase ethnic tensions, generate conflicts and promote separatism. All these have eroded any gains against ethnocentrism from liberal capitalism (another important legacy of the West in Africa). It has been observed that ethnocratic considerations override macro-economic prudence, as governments engage in practices that impede proper policy formulation and implementation.

Manyasa advocates for ethnic cohesion, especially in the Border States. In the case of East Africa, he sees the cross-border ethnic cohesion as presenting a grand opportunity for regional integration. He also advocates for a situation where there is the creation of institutions and systems of governance that recognise ethnic diversity and protect the diverse ethnic interests. For him, if this is done, ethnicity then could be a great opportunity for Africa's social, economic and political development. He says that until and unless ethnicity is recognised as the most salient factor in the peace and stability of Africa, sustainable development will continue to elude this continent.

Mohammed Kulumba on Ethno-Centralism and Movement Politics in Uganda discusses the local council 2002 elections in Kibaale, which is one of the most hetero-ethnic districts in Uganda. The bone of contention is that a 'Mukiiga immigrant' was elected the chairperson of the district. The indigenous people (the Bunyoro) of the district however rejected the results of these elections. This whole electoral process consequently sparked off bloody and destructive ethnic clashes between the indigenous Banyoro and the immigrant ethnic communities within the area. The violence in the area was unexpected in the sense that it took place at a time that was least expected: the Movement political system under which Uganda was governed had within the 16 years of its existence, been working towards the elimination of ethnic-based conflict. In an attempt to analyse this baffling ethnic conflict in Kibaale, Kulumba quotes Syahuka-Muhindo (1993) who argues that historical grievances, which are often articulated through ethnic explosions, build up over a long period of time. The State in its efforts to resolve the problem often appoints commissions and academicians who instead of looking at the root causes of the ethnic violence, which are historical, are more concerned with probing the ethnic violence itself.

Kulumba thus concludes that in order to understand and interpret the ethnic conflict in Kibaale, we must first and foremost analyse the history and contradic-tions within the Movement ideology, politics, policies and practice, and bring out the link between these and the conflict in Kibaale. For him, the conflict in Kibaale offers a perfect model for analysis in terms of the relationships between ethnocentrism and the electoral processes under the Movement ideology and practice. In fact, he blames the Kibaale conflict on the contradictions between the theory, policies and practice of the Movement politics, which work towards legitimising the Movement Government. He suggests the way forward, as the Movement Government ensuring an enabling environment where individuals and groups can participate in the political process on their own terms, but within the universally accepted rules. Given the background of the Movement Government, he however wonders if it is capable of providing this environment to its people.

Bahru Zewde, in his paper, Intellectuals and soldiers: The socialist experiment in the horn of Africa, attempts to describe and analyse the record of Marxist-Leninist regime in the horn, by focusing on its ideology, organisation and politics. He specifically draws attention to the ascendancy of the Marxist-Leninist doctrine in the insurgent forces in the region, such as the Eritrean Popular Liberation Front (EPLF) in Eritrea and the Tigray people's Liberation Front (TPLF) in Ethiopia. In a comparative framework, Zewde also draws on the insurgent regime in Lusophone Africa and the Marxist military regimes of Benin and Congo. In his discussions, he observes that even though the African leaders were reluctant to fully embrace the tenets of scientific socialism or Marxism-Leninism, Socialism actually had a resource among African leaders during their struggle for independence, since it was an ideology of liberation. They thus sought to ground socialism in the allegedly egalitarian and communalistic traditions of pre-colonial Africa. This saw the emergence of African Socialism in the 1960s.

Zewde concludes that even though African socialism and Marxism-Leninism eventually failed to have a long lasting impact in Africa, this did not mean that the factors which led to their temporary appeal and ascendancy were/are no longer there and relevant. Apart from these factors, he insists that Africa has still to define and redefine its relationship with the global order that controls its destiny both in the past, and continues to dominate even today. Within the objectives of Pan Africanism, Africa would therefore need an ideology that is not ossified into dogmatism, and a pragmatism that does not degenerate into opportunism.

Maurice Amutabi discusses Transient mobile 'Nations', and the dilemma of Nationhood in the Horn of Africa. He poses very many pertinent questions and seeks answers to them within the context of Globalisation. His paper is thus both a historical and philosophical interrogation of questions of Nationhood and Nationalism vis-à-vis the mobile nature of these nomadic pastoralists 'nations', which he discusses. For him, the common denominator in the transient or mobile character of these pastoralists is livestock. He therefore contends that in order to understand the characteristics and nature of pastoralists ethnic groups of the Horn, then one has got to examine livestock as both a commodity and a cultural artefact with its attendant attributes. He points out that the Horn of Africa and its environs is just an arena or theatre of sorts, in which greater global issues and rivalries have been, and continue to be played out, and that livestock are mere catalysts and pawns in the whole game.

Citing numerous examples from the region, Amutabi demonstrates that in as much as the problems of the Horn of Africa may be about livestock, they are also about ideological scheming and counter-scheming, and should be recognised as such. In his concluding remarks, Amutabi makes certain recommendations for the region. He advises all the governments in the region to be fully committed to the eradication of conflict in the region (although some Governments cannot be blamed since they do not have full control of the pastoral areas). Apart from an increase in military garrisons and police posts in the adjacent areas of the conflicts, armed village vigilante groups should also be encouraged. At the same time, the Government(s) concerned should lead in the process of disarming the pastoralists when they finally attain full control of them. The Government(s) should introduce sophisticated methods of branding, labelling and identification of animals, which will help in the tracking down of stolen animals. He also recommends that the NGOs and CBOs be given more leeway in bringing about peace in the region through mediation, conflict resolution and poverty reduction strategies. He contends that all these activities and efforts will go a long way in bringing about a sense of normalcy, peace and stability in these pastoralist areas.

Mohammed Kulumba in his second paper examines how the National Resistant Movement (NRM) has transformed from a movement of No-party political system, into a political party after it captured state power in Uganda in 1986. He argues that this transformation is as risky as what he calls 'riding on the tiger's back'. This is especially so, when the whole situation is seen against the backdrop of the history of the NRM, its original ideological orientation, legal basis and practical politics in the last 18 years. In this paper, Kulumba thus makes a critical analysis of the political and legal dilemma facing the NRM in its trans-formation, and suggests the way forward for a transformational process from a movement into a political party. He warns that unless fundamental issues are systematically and effectively addressed, then Uganda may slip back into political instability and violence that had characterised its entire post-independence period.

Among other questions, Kulumba asks if the Political Party and Organisa-tion Act of 2002 contains sufficient legal framework to allow competitive multi-party politics in Uganda; whether there is any contradiction between the NRM Constitution and the Political parties and Organisation Act 2002; and to what extent the NRM has involved the people of Uganda in its transformation. He argues that the NRM transformation to a political organisation was an 'internal evolution' or mechanism to continue their hold on power in the absence of an alternative. Given the illegalities and the political dilemma facing NRM transfor-mation and its long established desire for political dominance, it is difficult to see the proper functioning of a multi-party system in Uganda in the short-term. Kulumba concludes that it is now up to Ugandans to ensure that the step taken by NRM is the right step. Fundamentally, Ugandans have to struggle for more steps towards a genuine, competitive multi-party system in Uganda. The con-verse would mean that all Ugandans, and not only the NRM would be taking a ride on the back of a tiger.

Looking at the different dimensions of the challenges confronting the countries of the East African region, particular effort is made not to neglect the weak points or blind spots of the theory and practice of African nationalism, taking full cognisance of the changed contexts and conditions shaping the African world today. The book thus reflects on different dimensions of these challenges, the various strands of reform being pursued and their potential for establishing the foundations for the emergence of an inclusive, democratic and developmental State system. The various contributions in this book therefore provide alternative readings of the problems confronting the sub-region and alternative approaches to meeting these challenges. CODESRIA hopes that this collection of essays is able to enrich policy, scholarship and understanding of East Africans and their Pan-African aspirations.

1

The Rise, the Fall and the Insurrection of Nationalism in Africa

Issa G. Shivji

Argument

We have become so used to the rhetoric of the 'global village' that talking about nationalism sounds anachronistic and outdated. But that is exactly what I am going to talk about. In this presentation, I want to explore the 'National Question' and its erstwhile expression; nationalism. The presentation is in three sections. First, the rise of post-war nationalism and its true essence, if you like; then the debunking of nationalism in the post-Cold War period under the apparent hegemony of neo-liberalism and the so-called globalisation. Finally, still holding high the Gramscian adage, 'pessimism of the intellect, optimism of the will', I anticipate an insurrection of second nationalism.

The Post-War Nationalism

The Essence of Nationalism

Introducing his book *Freedom and After* (1963), Tom Mboya recalls what he calls, the 'proudest day of my life'. That day was December 6th, 1958, the day of the opening of the All Africa Peoples Conference in Accra, Ghana. Earlier in the same year there had been a conference of independent African states. There were only eight at the time. 'These two conferences', says Mboya, 'marked the rediscovery of Africa by Africans.' He continues:

> ...[T]his rediscovery of Africa by Africans was 'in complete contrast to the discovery of Africa by Europeans in the nineteenth century'. The Conference of Independent African States had marked the birth of the African personality, and the delegates had all agreed on the need for Africa to rise and be heard at all the councils of the world affairs (Mboya: 1963: 13-14).

Some five hundred delegates attended the conference from political parties, trade unions and others involved in the great awakening that was nationalism. Patrice Lumumba and Roberto Holden were there, and so was Dr. Kamuzu Banda. The nationalist upsurge in the post-war period in Africa was the great moment for a people who had been denied humanity by centuries of slavery and colonialism. Ideologies surrounding Kwame Nkrumah's 'African Personality' or Senghor's 'Negritude' or Kaunda's 'Humanism' or even Nyerere's *Ujamaa* expressed essentially one central theme, nationalism. The quintessence of nationalism was, and is, anti-imperialism. It was a demand and struggle against, rather than for something. It was an expression of a struggle against denial; denial of humanity, denial of respect and dignity, denial of the Africanness of the African. It was the struggle for the 're-Africanisation of minds' or to 'rebecome Africans' as Amilcar Cabral put it (Cabral 1980:xxii, xxv). Archie Mafeje sums it well when he says:

> It was the historical experience of racial humiliation, economic exploitation, political oppression and cultural domination under European and American slavery, colonialism and imperialism, that gave rise to theories of 'African personality' and 'Negritude'. At the centre of these theories was the question of the liberation of the Black man, his identity or the meaning of 'being-Black-in-the-world'. It was a philosophical or moral justification for action, for a rebellion, which gave rise to African nationalism and to independence. The later was the greatest political achievement by Africans. It was an unprecedented collective fulfilment... (Mafeje 1992:11-12).

This nationalism should not be confused with the traditional discourse on expression and development of nations in the womb of capitalism in the nineteenth century Europe. Rather, it was an expression of a *people* as an antidote to white supremacist rule. In a sense, it is correct to say that nationalism was the process; a process of struggle in the formation of nations. In that sense, perhaps, nationalism preceded nations. Militant nationalists grasped this *to some extent* although they did not express it as consistently nor did they wholly appreciate the defining characteristic of nationalism; that is, anti-imperialism. Nyerere, explaining the objectives of the Tanganyika African National Union (or TANU) to the United Nations Trusteeship Council in 1955 said:

> Another objective of the Union is to build up a national consciousness among the African peoples in Tanganyika. It has been said - and this is quite right - that Tanganyika is tribal, and we realise that we need to break up this tribal consciousness among the people and to build up a national consciousness. That is one of our main objectives towards self-government (Nyerere 1967:38-39).

This formulation is no doubt problematic. It lends itself to the reactionary aspect of bourgeois nationalism, or what later came to be called 'nation-building theories' (see Wamba-dia-Wamba in Shivji 1991:57-70). Let us look at another formulation, this time from a leading member of a national liberation movement and an avowed Marxist; Marcelino Dos Santos, then a leading member of FRELIMO. In an interview with Joe Slovo of the South African Communist Party, Dos Santos analyses the tension between tribe and nation, thus:

> The main conditions for (the) successful rejection (of tribalism) are present. On the general point of whether we have already moulded a nation in the true sense of the word, I want to say that a nation is based on concrete realities. And the most important reality in the present stage in Mocambique is the fight against Portuguese colonialism... It is our common fight against our common oppressor, which plays an outstanding role in creating a national bond between all the diverse groups and cultures... Of course a nation is a product of history and its formation goes through different phases. In this sense, the work for the final achievement of nationhood will continue even after independence although the fundamental elements of nationhood are already in existence and in the process of being further developed in Mocambique. (Quoted in Slovo in Diepen 1988:144).

This conception of national-formation is not fundamentally different from Nyerere's presentation of 'nation-building', although their points of departure are supposedly different. Dos Santos, like Joe Slovo who quotes him, takes the Marxist theory of nation (presumably this is 'the true sense of the word') as his point of departure which, in its Stalinist version, overemphasises the European version of 'what is a nation' - common territory, common language, culture, economy etc. If all these ingredients are not present, or not present in sufficient degree, you have a tribe, at worst, or a nation in formation, at best. Implied in this is also the conception of voluntarism; that is, forming or building of a nation from the top. Perhaps the important point to underline in Dos Santos's exposition is the element of anti-colonial *struggle* as an important ingredient of nationalism. The problem with Santos- and Nyerere-type formulations was that when in power, the nationalist petty bourgeoisie wavered on anti-imperialism and ended up with top-down statist projects of 'nation-building'.

I find Amilcar Cabral's propositions more fruitful. They contain a germ of great potential in understanding the historicity and specificity of the 'national question' in Africa. Among a number of his formulation on nationalism, Cabral says that nationalism was a struggle not only to reclaim history, but also to assert the right of the African people to make history, '... the foundation of national liberation lies in the inalienable right of every people to have their own history, ...' (Cabral 1980:143). The second idea in Cabral is that 'so long as imperialism is in existence, an independent African state must be a liberation movement in power, or it will not be independent.' (1980:116). These are profound insights. First, that nationalism is constituted by the *struggle of the people* against imperialism. Thus anti-imperialism is what defines nationalism. Second, that nationalism, as an expression of struggle, continues so long as imperialism exists. Therefore, thirdly, the 'National Question' in Africa, whose expression is nationalism, remains unresolved so long as there is imperialist domination. It is these insights, which I find drawn out succinctly by Archie Mafeje in his various writings which need to be synthesised and interrogated.

Mafeje observes that 'all the struggles in Africa and most of the Third World centre on the National Question' and that the common denominator underlying different meanings and connotations of the National Question is nationalism. Furthermore, he says, 'nationalism is always a reaction against something. In African history, nationalism has been a reaction against imperialist domination. First, as proto-nationalism, it was against the colonial phase of imperialism, which was mainly concerned with political domination by aliens. In the post-independence phase, meta-nationalism is concerned much more with the changing modalities of imperialist domination' (Mafeje 1992:90). These insights by Mafeje are, in my view, extremely important and need to be deepened further.

Now, this has not been the dominant discourse on the National Question. Both from the right and the left, the central element in the National Question has been the question of the existence or otherwise of the 'nation' rather than nationalism. Thus the whole debate on whether or not Africa has nations and nationalities, as opposed to tribes and ethnic groups (cf. the debates among the Ethiopian and the South African Left, Diepen 1988). In the Euro centric worldview, of course, nations and nationalities represent a higher level in the evolution of social and political formations as compared to tribes. Fed on Stalin's rather schematic formula, and therefore unable to find nations within the territorial units called countries, even radical Marxists have found it difficult to theorise adequately the National Question (see, for example, Slovo 1988). In the hands of right-wing pundits, it has been worse. The so-called lack of nations has been used to debunk and delegitimise nationalist movements and their achievements. In the current hegemony of neo-liberalism and imperial comeback, the spokespersons of imperialism have been quick to condemn nationalisms as nothing more than expressions of ethnicity and tribalism. Here is a typical sample from the editorial in *US News and World Report*:

> In the Third World, there had been grand ideas of new states and social contracts among the communities, post-colonial dreams of what men and women could do on their own. There were exalted notions of Indian nationalism, Pan-Arabism and the like. Ethnicity hid, draped in the colours of modern nationalism, hoping to keep the ancestors - and the troubles – at

bay. But the delusions would not last. What was India? The India of its secular founders – or the 'Hindu Raj' of the militant fundamentalists? What exactly did the compact communities of Iraq – the Kurds, the Sunnis and the Shia – have in common? The masks have fallen, the tribes have stepped to the fore (Quoted in Furedi 1994:102).

This type of denigration strikes at the heart of nationalism, that is, anti-imperialism. Be that as it may, let us look more closely at the expressions and aspects of nationalism.

Three Aspects of Nationalism

There are three elements, which characterised proto-nationalism and which, with different emphasis, accent and formulation, recur in nationalist thought and consciousness. The three elements are: Pan-Africanism, Independence or Freedom and (Racial) Equality. Each one of these, and all three together, are asserted against their denial and, therefore, in opposition to something; in this case, imperial domination. And this assertion, this struggle, is what constitutes nationalism, albeit with different content during different historical periods, as Mafeje says, but remaining a common principle. The gravamen of the National Question therefore, is not so much a nation in search of, or struggling for identity, dignity, and independence, but rather a people imbued with a common experience of domination and exploitation asserting its 'claim-in-struggle'. *It is this – that is anti-imperialism – which happens to be the essence of nationalism.*

The three aspects of nationalism, which may be summed up as Unity, Equality and Independence, are inter-related and inseparable. Together they constitute and express nationalism. In the hands of Kwame Nkrumah, who studied in the US and was heavily influenced by such African-American giants as George Padmore, C.L.R. James and others, Pan-Africanism expressed the identity or the Africanness of both the peoples on the continent and in the Diaspora. For someone like Nyerere, as he himself was to admit later, Pan-Africanism essentially meant African unity (see Interview with Ikaweba Bunting in The Internationalist, December 1988). Whatever the scope, nationalism was, and I might add is, incomplete without Pan-Africanism. Nyerere expressed this idea presciently as long ago as 1963 when he said; 'African nationalism is meaningless, is anachronistic, and is dangerous, if it is not at the same time Pan-Africanism.' (Nyerere 1966:194).

In the immediate post-independence period, Pan-Africanism resolved itself into two elements; African Unity, expressed in the formation of the OAU, and support of the liberation movements in the remaining colonies, including South Africa. In spite of various problems, as Nyerere was to point out, 'We have been reasonably successful in achieving the second purpose [that is in ending colonialism]. But as far as uniting Africa is concerned, we have not succeeded.' ('Dialogue with Nyerere' in Sandbrook & Halfani 1993:25).

The other element; freedom or independence, was primarily concerned with anti-colonialism; that is against alien domination. This is the aspect that was most fulfilled in the independence of African countries. But independence or freedom also had another deeper significance, and that is the freedom or the right to make one's own decisions; that is the right to self-determination. The external aspect of the right of self-determination is expressed in the sovereignty of the state. While independence meant that the African state was formally sovereign in international law, in practice, its independence and sovereignty were heavily circumscribed. The Cold War added fuel to the fire. Nationalist leaders who took their independence seriously became the potential target of imperial wrath. Patrice Lumumba was assassinated. Kwame Nkrumah was overthrown. Thomas Sankara was killed. Nyerere survived by tactical compromises and by nipping in the bud potential local opposition. When he was asked to name his greatest achievement after ten years of the Arusha Declaration, he said, perhaps with a deep sigh of relief, 'The fact that we have survived.' (Interview with Peter Enahoro, *Africa Now*).

The third aspect of nationalism; equality, involves several interrelated levels. First, equal treatment of states, whether big or small, weak or strong at international level in world councils. This, as every one knows, is spurious - some are more equal than others. Yet, in solidarity with other Third World countries, militant African nationalists did manage to carve out a respectable place for themselves and their peoples in the discourse on the inequalities of the imperial world market and International Financial Institutions. Non-alignment, UNCTAD conferences, several UN Conventions and Resolutions in their favour, were some kind of achievement, albeit very limited.

There is the other element of equality. This is internal. Equality and equal rights are the cornerstone of bourgeois legal system and liberal democracy. In many independent states, barring military dictatorships and settler colonies, formal equality was installed as colonial racial privileges were dismantled. But that is where it attenuated. For various reasons, even civilian African states became authoritarian expressing their rule in rightless law and one-party states (see Shivji in Shivji 1991:27–56).

But bourgeois equality, as every one knows, has severe limitations. It is always in tension with equity and social justice, which may require the negation of formal equality. In the African condition, it is lack of equity underlying enormous inequalities that made nonsense of any formal equality. And the socio-economic condition underlying inequalities and inequities were in no small measure connected with imperial domination, in its neo-colonial phase.

The petty bourgeoisie in power quickly differentiate and fail to address the 'National Question' in all its aspects because they fail, to use once again, Cabral's phrase, to be 'a liberation movement in power'. The class is compradorised, through and through. The damning condemnation of the 'national bourgeoisie', as he called it, came from none other than that great paragon of nationalism, Frantz Fanon (1963):

> The national middle class discovers its historic mission: that of intermediary. Seen through its eyes, its mission has nothing to do with transforming the nation; it consists, prosaically, of being the transmission line between the nation and a capitalism, rampant though camouflaged, which today puts on the masque of neo-colonialism... In the colonial countries, the spirit of indulgence is dominant at the core of the bourgeoisie; and this is because the national bourgeoisie identifies itself with the western bourgeoisie, from whom it has learnt its lessons. It follows the Western bourgeoisie along its path of negation and decadence without ever having emulated it in its first stages of exploration and invention, stages that are an acquisition of that Western bourgeoisie whatever the circumstances. In its beginnings, the national bourgeoisie of the colonial countries identifies itself with the decadence of the bourgeoisie of the West. We need not think that it is jumping ahead; it is in fact beginning at the end. It is already senile before it has come to know the petulance, the fearlessness or the will to succeed of youth (Fanon 1963: 122–123).

So the 'National Question' remains unresolved. Nation building turns into state building. Nation is substituted by party and the party by the leader; the father of the nation. As Wamba-dia-Wamba puts it; 'The commonality which is viewed as the foundation of "national consciousness" is reduced to its phenomenal expressions: cultural unity, territorial unity, linguistic unity, "one classless community', "one people, one party, one leader, father figure, father of the nation", etc.' (Wamba 1991:61, & Wamba 1996 in Olukoshi & Laakso 1996).

If the 'National Question' was distorted, truncated and caricatured during the period of meta-nationalism, it completely disappears and is delegitimised in the globalisation phase of imperialism. The 'National Question' is reduced to the race or ethnic question or to the cultural question. In my country, the journalistic discourse has transformed from *utaifa* (nationalism) or *uzalendo* (patriotism) to *uzawa* (indigenity)! Meanwhile, the leader harangues us on to change, to move with the times, to embrace globalisation, to be members of the 'global village' while villages are privatised and villagers marginalized, and the global pillage marches on unabashed. The comprador bourgeoisie, as always, is being led by the nose by the imperial bourgeoisie. In the next section, we discuss how nationalism – both proto and meta – is being annihilated by the assault of imperialism in the new garb of globalisation.

The Neo-Liberal Assault on Nationalism

Recently, addressing the parliamentary foreign affairs committee of my country, the United States ambassador commended Tanzania for the change in its foreign policy from that based on principles of 'African Freedom and African Unity' (Nyerere 1967:2) to that based on 'economic diplomacy'. He said:

> The liberation diplomacy of the past, when alliances with socialist nations were paramount and so-called Third World Solidarity dominated foreign policy, must give way to a more realistic approach to dealing with your true friends – those who are working to lift you into the 21st century where poverty is not acceptable and disease must be conquered (*The Guardian*, 29 July 2003).

In this, the representative of the super imperial power is, in no uncertain terms, debunking the nationalist planks of the independence era. He is assuming that the imperial power has the right to determine for our countries our friends and enemies, as indeed they are doing. In the spate of the so-called anti-terrorism laws thrust by the US upon African countries, it is the US and its cohorts - the so-called international community - who determine who is a terrorist and what is a terrorist organisation (see the Prevention of Terrorism Act, 2002, of Tanzania). This is a far cry from the nationalism of leaders like Nyerere who could say, 'We will not allow our friends to choose enemies for us'.

As the Berlin Wall fell and imperialism began to take the offensive, Douglas Hurd, then the British Secretary of State for Foreign Affairs, sighed with relief that 'we are putting behind us a period of history when the West was unable to express a legitimate interest in the developing world without being accused of "neo-colonialism"' (quoted in Furedi 1994:99). One of the most articulate and fervent nationalists against neo-colonialism was of course Kwame Nkrumah. His book *Neo-colonialism: The Last Stage of Imperialism* (1965) reverberated throughout the continent. Imperialism never forgave him for that. As is known, a year after the publication of the book, Nkrumah was overthrown in a CIA-organised coup.

The political assault on nationalism in what Furedi calls the 'moral rehabilitation of imperialism' is accompanied and rationalised by the 'organic' intellectuals and paid journalists of imperial powers. The basic claim is that Third World Nationalism, and African nationalism in particular, was spurious as its collapse, according to the pundits, amply proves. According to this thought, there is an upsurge of 'ethnic nationalism' and primordial tribal wars tearing African states apart resulting in failed states, collapsed states, or in a more sophisticated language, the crisis of the nation-state. As astute and sympathetic an observer of Africa as Basil Davidson sees the nation-state as the *Black Man's Burden* (Davidson 1992). So, because the nation-state has become a curse, presumably the African should return to the blessing of his (it certainly wasn't 'hers'!) idyllic past.

Central to the nationalist project, as we have seen, was the right of the people to self-determination (see Shivji 2002). This was the assertion of the people's collective right to assert their identity and determine their own destiny. Opposed to the paradigm based on the self-determination of the collective, 'people' are the various variants of post-modernism premised on the *self-determination of the individual*. The universal individual is opposed to the African individual, never mind that in reality the universal individual is in fact the Western individual. Africanity and Africanness are demeaned, if not demonised, as the so-called 'victimhood' mentality of the African and the parochial and self-fulfilling discourse of the African intellectual, made in myth rather than reality, are roundly condemned (Mbembe 2000). The ultimate in this free-floating, self-determining individual is Mbembe's frivolous narrative in which 'in the future, everyone can imagine and choose what makes him or her an African' (ibid., 10). But I need say no more on this apparently self-denying and yet utterly narcissistic, vituperation. Mafeje has given it a simple but fitting reply. 'The free-floating signifier' says Mafeje, 'is an illusion in a double sense. First, nobody can think and act outside historically determined circumstances and still hope to be a social signifier of any kind.' Secondly, 'it is the historical juncture which defines us socially and intellectually.' (Mafeje 2000: 66). And for Mafeje, like a number of others, the historical juncture remains that of the unresolved 'national question.'

But I am running ahead of my story. Let me return to the more mainstream and prevalent discourse of the 'universal being' in the universal condition of the neo-liberal's globalisation. In the flattened imagery of the 'global village', we have the good forces of globalisation poised to rescue the African villager from the mismanagement and bad governance of the corrupt, patrimonial state ruled by avaricious politicians who know no politics except that of the belly.[1] The state, the nation, the people and their historical national and contemporary social struggles are all dismissed from the paradigm or rhetorically condemned as misguided projects. This does not stop at the rhetoric. Sophisticated discourses are constructed to vindicate the debunking of the nationalist project and its social and political basis.

In a series of paradigmatic shifts, the meta-narratives, the political discourse and the social science analysis of the national question are systematically undermined. Civil society is opposed to the state, both presented as institutional formations rather than an ensemble of social and power relations. The state is condemned, civil society is acclaimed. National liberation movements and class-based organisations like the trade unions or peasant associations are considered outdated, while NGOs, run by free-floating 'activists', are privileged. Human rights discourse is presented as a neutral, universal, apolitical and ahistorical 'revelation', while a discourse on the oppression of peoples and nations is ridiculed as rhetorical and unworthy of science.

The so-called new breed leaders, from Meles Zenawi of Ethiopia, Isaias of Eritrea through Museveni to Mbeki and Mkapa are a caricatured local representation of the neo-liberal hegemony. 'African Renaissance' is worse than a pale copy of Kwame Nkrumah's 'African Personality', and utterly uninspiring. NEPAD comes nowhere close to the Lagos Plan of Action. It uses the same failed rhetoric of further integration in the so-called globalised world. It derives its legitimacy from the IFIs rather than the African people. It has attracted opposition from 'civil society' organisations, whose main thrust is to highlight anti-globalisation (Bond 2002). There is very little nationalist content to NEPAD.

Ironically, the equality of all countries and states in the OAU and non-interference in the internal affairs and sentiments of Pan-Africanism maintained some relative peace among them. Since the advent of 'new breed' globalised leaders however, we have had African wars and invasions as in the Congo, between Eritrea and Ethiopia and in West Africa. Today, under the guise of UN–US peace-keeping, we are witnessing the rise of regional 'super-powers' sponsored, armed and financed by imperialism. The Pan-African ideal does not even enjoy lip service among these proponents of 'African Renaissance'.

In sum, the neo-liberal discourse and political rhetoric have served to debunk nationalism on the one hand, and rehabilitate imperialism on the other. Intellectually, the majority of African intellectuals have been pretty well accommodated in the mainstream. This includes the former militant nationalists and radical socialist intellectuals. The metamorphosis of the African intellectual from the revolutionary to the activist; from the critical political economist to post-modernist; from the social analyst to constitutionalist liberal; from an anti-imperialist to a cultural activist, from a radical economics professor to a neo-liberal World Bank spokesperson, from an intellectual to a consultant, is blatant, unrepentant and mercenary. Yet it is ephemeral. The stream of more radical, more committed and a more militant and insurrectionary intellectual thought continues to flow. It is to this that I turn next in an effort to explore how the 'National Question' can be rearticulated and reconfigured with the democratic and social questions.

The National, the Democratic and the Social Question

The State of the Discourse

At the end of a Symposium on Marxism held in Dar es Salaam in 1983 to celebrate the centenary of Marx's death, the conclusion was: 'The Central Question of the African Revolution Today is Democracy.' The rise of the authoritarian state and the statisation of civil society in the post-colonial period, elicited the democracy discourse in the 1980s and 1990s. This dovetailed into the collapse of the Soviet empire, the end of the Cold War and the comeback of Western imperialism under the US. As neo-liberal discourse in economics was generalised to politics, the dominant democracy debate began to centre around liberal paradigms - constitutionalism, human rights, and the restructuring of the state in the image of liberal states (Shivji 1990). In the first phase of the democracy debate, Left intellectuals began to revisit the actually existing experience of the struggles of their people. Fine volumes like the *Popular Struggles for Democracy in Africa* edited by Anyang' Nyongo (1987), and *African Studies in Social Movements and Democracy* edited by Mahmood Mamdani and Ernest Wamba-dia-Wamba (1995), were produced.[2] These works were still rooted in the methodology of radical political economy, yet critically interrogating it and in the process, deepening the understanding of our societies. The democracy question was not abstracted from history and its social character. What is more, the then prevalent notions of abstract civil society, class-less community and apolitical NGOs were convincingly debunked. Thus social movements were firmly conceptualised and presented as social struggles, nay, class struggles (see Mamdani's Introduction to *Social Movements...*).

The same cannot be said of the African scholars' intellectual activity in the 1990s, including that of the Left intellectual. If the African ruling class has been even more de-nationalised and compradorised in this phase of globalisation, the African (Left) intellectual has been liberalised, and perhaps even compromised. The globalisation and neo-liberal discourse on constitutionalism, rights and democracy has proved to be overwhelming. The rights discourse has been so much hegemonised, that when I produced a slim volume in the late 1980s (Shivji 1989) arguing that the human rights discourse was an ideology constructed historically within the dominant imperialism, I was roundly condemned by my left comrades as demagogic! As fine a Leftist a scholar as Mamdani declared: 'Wherever there was (and is) oppression, there must come into being a conception of rights.' (Mamdani 1991 in Shivji 1991:237). Now it may be true that wherever there is oppression, there is bound to be resistance; à la Mao, but it is simply not true that that resistance necessarily takes the form of rights, meaning equal rights as in the bourgeois construct. Be that as it may, the point I am making is simply that the ahistorical and asocial human rights and democracy discourse has taken toll of Left scholars as well. And one of these 'tolls' has been the increasing disappearance of the National Question from our democracy discourse.

There is no doubt that democracy is the central question of the African Revolution today. But the question is how is this related to, or configured with the National and Social Question? This is because neither the National Question nor the Democracy Question can be addressed or interrogated outside its social character and much less, can it be resolved outside class struggle; the locomotive of history.

'Come Back Africa'

While I may have talked bitterly about the conversion of African intellectuals to neo-liberalism, the picture is no doubt overdrawn to make the point. One is allowed to exaggerate the truth, so long as you are not telling lies! The truth is that in the people's own struggle, the national question and nationalism in the sense of anti-imperialism and anti-compradorism, are being brought back on the historical agenda. These struggles may be local and disparate; they may be issue-oriented and articulated in ways and ideologies, sometimes parochial, sometimes even religious, yet the resistance and rebellion against the new and old compradors is in the making. It is these that the intellectuals need to investigate, research, expose, articulate and systematise and theorise about.

Similarly, our own intellectuals, and by this I mean CODESRIA intellectuals, albeit few, have been agonising over the present state of affairs. Numbers do not matter. 'Better fewer but better.' Samir Amin and Archie Mafeje have consistently argued their positions from the vantage point of political economy, posing a new alliance of popular classes and forces which may take forward the anti-imperialist and anti-comprador national project.[3] Mafeje has rightly continued to underscore the importance of the National Question and has insightfully combined with it the Democratic and Social Question. He has insisted on concrete identification of social forces in concrete African conditions so as to determine what kind of democracy is at issue on the continent. He offers certain tentative, yet insightful, observations, which may be further developed (Mafeje 1995).

Let me offer a few thoughts, which I presented in an article at an international conference in Dar es Salaam marking the 75th birthday of Mwalimu Julius Nyerere. I argued for a new national democratic consensus in Africa that would be thoroughly popular, thoroughly anti-imperialist and thoroughly anti-comprador (Shivji 2000). I suggested three cornerstones as critical in constructing a new consensus: popular livelihoods, popular participation and popular power. I use the term "popular" to signify three things. First, popular is used in the sense of being anti-imperialist. Imperialism is the negation of both 'national' and 'democratic', but I use the term popular to transcend the limits of the term 'national', which signified anti-colonialism. Independence or first liberation consisted in constituting state sovereignty; the core of the second liberation consists in resolving the issue of people's sovereignty.

The second meaning of popular refers to the social basis of the new consensus or nationalism. The social core of the new consensus has to be popular classes or a popular bloc of classes. The exact composition of the popular bloc would of course differ, but in many African countries, the land-based producer classes and the urban working people together with lower middle classes would constitute the 'masses'. This is where, to use Lenin's phrase, 'serious politics begin' – 'not where there are thousands, but where there are millions' (quoted in Carr 1961:50).

The third meaning of popular refers to popular perceptions, custom, culture and consciousness. Custom and culture, not in the vulgar sense of atrophied and unchanging tradition, but in the sense of a living terrain of struggles where the old and the new, the progressive and the reactionary, jostle and struggle to attain hegemony. This is the sense that is brought out in Cabral's great premise that 'national liberation is necessarily an act of culture' (Cabral 1980:143).

I shall not go on. These are only tentative pointers. The point simply is to argue for, even to anticipate an insurrection of new nationalism to counter imperialism in its globalisation phase, which is at the same time deeply anti-compradorial so as to resolve the National Question and, hopefully, pave the way for social emancipation. I will end with a poem *Come Back, Africa* written by Faiz Ahmed Faiz in 1955, heralding the coming of the first African nationalism. May it also herald the second nationalism.

Come, your drum-beats echo in my soul,
the rhythm of my blood rings, Come Back Africa!
From dust of humiliation have I raised my head,
wiped sorrow-crust off my eyes,
Liberated my arms from pain,
And torn the net of helplessness, Come, Africa!
Each crooked ring of fetters which bound me
is now an armoury in firm grip,
I have broken the halter round my neck and
moulded into a shield.
My spear-heads like the eyes of wild deers,
Surround him in all our dens,
And the dark of night is red with enemy blood,
The very heart of earth beats with my heart, Africa!
Rivers thrill, and forests tremble,
I am Africa now, I incarnate you, Africa,
Like your lions walk,
Come Africa, Come with the stride of a lion,
Come Back Africa![4]

Notes

1. A play on the title of Bayart's book, *The Politics of the Belly* (1993).
2. A number of country-specific studies in the same vein were also produced by CODESRIA's National Working Groups. I had the privilege of editing one on Tanzania called *The State and the Working People in Tanzania* (1986). It is heartening to note that these works were sponsored and published by our leading Pan-African and Third World organisations, CODESRIA and the

Third World Forum, which many African scholars have been proud to be associated with.

3. It is unfortunate that in his magnum opus, *Citizens and Subjects*, Mahmood Mamdani abandons political economy too radically and falls into an institutional analysis of the colonial state. He thus arrives at the finding that the colonial state was bifurcated, when an examination of its social character would have revealed the unity of state power. While his conclusions on the tasks of democratic struggle are unassailable, his preceding institutional analysis results in his 'recommendation' for the reform of state structures rather than positing of a new form of nationalist struggle. Throughout his analysis, Mamdani concentrates on the 'native question', the preoccupation of the colonial power, but has little to say about the 'national question', the preoccupation of the resistance. This work needs much closer analysis than what I can offer in these few remarks.

4. Originally written in Urdu, translated into English by Sajjad Zahir and published in *New Age* (weekly), Delhi, October 9, 1955. I have taken it from Mukherjee (1985).

References

Bayart, J. F., 1993, *The State in Africa: The Politics of the Belly*, New York: Longman.

Bond, P., ed., 2002, F*anon's Warning: a Civil Society Reader on the New Partnership for Africa's Development*, New Jersey: Africa World Press.

Cabral, A., 1980, *Unity and Struggle: Speeches and Writings*, London: Heinemann.

Carr, E. H. 1961, *What is History?* London: Penguin.

Davidson, B., 1992, *The Black Man's Burden: Africa and the Curse of the Nation-State*, New York: Times Books, Random House.

Fanon, F., 1963, *The Wretched of the Earth*, London:Penguin.

Furedi, F., 1994, *The New Ideology of Imperialism*, London: Pluto Press.

Mafeje, A., 1992, *In Search of an Alternative: A Collection of Essays on Revolutionary Theory and Politics*, Harare: SAPES.

Mafeje, A., 1995, 'Theory of Democracy and the African Discourse: Breaking Bread with my Fellow-Travellers', in E. Chole & Jibrin Ibrahim (eds.), *Democratisation Processes in Africa: Problems and Prospects*, Dakar: CODESRIA.

Mafeje, A., 2000, 'Africanity: A Combative Ontology', *CODESRIA Bulletin*, Number 1, 2000.

Mamdani, M., & Wamba-dia-Wamba, E., eds., 1995, *African Studies in Social Movements and Democracy*, Dakar: CODESRIA.

Mamdani, M., 1991, 'Social Movements and Constitutionalism in the African Context', in Issa G. Shivji, (ed.) *State and Constitutionalism: An African Debate on Democracy*, Harare: SAPES.

Mamdani, M., 1996, *Citizen and Subject: Contemporary Africa and the Legacy of Late Colonialism*, New Jersey: Princeton.

Mbembe, A., 2000, 'African Modes of Self-Writing', *CODESRIA Bulletin*, No. 1.

Mboya, T., 1963, *Freedom and After*, London: Andre Deutsch.

Mukherjee, R., 1985, *Uganda: An Historical Accident? Class, Nation, State Formation*, New Jersey: Africa World Press.

Nkrumah, K., 1965, *Neo-Colonialism: The Last Stage of Imperialism*, London: Heinemann.

Nyerere, J., 1967, 'Tanzania Policy on Foreign Affairs', Address at the Tanganyika African National Union National Conference, Mwanza, 16th October 1967.

Nyerere, J., 1967, *Freedom and Unity: A Selection from Writings and Speeches, 1952–65*, Dar es Salaam, OUP.

Nyongo, Anyang' P., ed., 1987, *Popular Struggles for Democracy in Africa*, London: Zed.

Sandbrook, R. & Halfani, Mohamed, eds., 1993, 'Socialism, Democracy and Development in Africa: A Dialogue with Mwalimu Julius K. Nyerere', in Sandbrook & Halfani (eds.) *Empowering People: Building Community, Civil Associations and Legality in Africa*, Toronto: Centre for Urban and Community Studies.

Shivji, I. G., 1989, *The Concept of Human Rights in Africa*, Dakar: CODESRIA.

Shivji, I. G., 1991, 'State and Constitutionalism: A New Democratic Perspective', in Issa G. Shivji, (ed.), *State and Constitutionalism: An African Debate on Democracy*, Harare: SAPES.

Shivji, I. G., 2000, 'Critical Elements of a New Democratic Consensus in Africa', in Haroub Othman (ed.) *Reflections on Leadership in Africa: Forty Years after Independence*, VUB University Press.

Shivji, I. G., 2002, 'Is Might a Right in International Human Rights? Notes on the Imperialist Assault on the Right of Peoples to Self-determination,' in Sifuni E. Mchome, (ed.) *Taking Stock of Human Rights Situation in Africa*, Dar es Salaam: Faculty of Law, University of Dar es Salaam.

Shivji, I. G., ed., 1986, *The State and the Working People in Tanzania*, Dakar: CODESRIA.

Slovo, J.,1988, 'The Working Class and Nation-Building', in Maria van Diepen (ed.) *The National Question in South Africa*, London: Zed Books.

The Guardian, 29th July 2003.

Wamba-dia-Wamba, E., 1991, 'Discourse on the National Question' in Issa G. Shivji, (ed.), *State and Constitutionalism: An African Debate on Democracy*, Harare, SAPES.

Wamba-dia-Wamba, E., 1996, 'The National Question in Zaire: Challenges to the Nation-State Project', in Adebayo O. Olukoshi and Liisa Laakso, (eds.), *Challenges to the Nation-State in Africa*, Uppsala, Nordic Africa Institute.

2

Intellectuals and Africa's Renewal*

Chachage Seithy L. Chachage

By Way of Introduction

I feel greatly elated and at the same time humbled to give a keynote speech to this Conference which has set itself the task of dealing with the difficult and elusive problem of Africa's predicament and the challenges regarding national and regional renewal. The task is even more daunting to me, given that I have to do so after A. Bujra and Z. Tadesse (who are closely associated with the founding of our Organisation—the Council for the Development of Social Science Research in Africa (CODESRIA)—and I. Shivji (who had already published *The Silent Class Struggles* by the time the organisation was founded), have said so much about the African intellectual community and CODESRIA's role over the years. When CODESRIA was founded in 1973, I was in secondary school (form IV). I did not know anything about this organisation until 1982, when I joined the University of Dar es Salaam as a Tutorial Assistant.

My intellectual growth, if I can say that, took place in the midst of the heat of the emergence of the New Right and the triumph of neo-liberalism world-wide, whose icons were Margaret Thatcher, Ronald Reagan and the current Roman Catholic Pope. It was a movement whose hallmark was the rolling back of the state as a development and social provisioning body and the cutting of funding for social services—including education and knowledge production. While still a student, even the fundamental objectives of the universities as academic institutions—scientific enquiry, pursuit of knowledge and the search of the whole truth (the consequence of that notwithstanding, without fear of the powers that be) in the interest of social transformation and human emancipation—were being relegated to the background. This undertaken in the name of certain notions of relevance; national (read state) interests, development needs, job market requirements, 'man-power' creation, etc). These are aspects which tended to reduce institutions of higher learning into mere government think-tanks and suppliers of high-level 'manpower' (women were forgotten) to the government and the private sector.

It was during the time when sophistry in the name of post-modernism, which was fighting tooth and nail against what it termed 'grand narratives' had become the intellectual fad. This was the trend that sought to fight against all attempts of humanity to attain fundamental truths that would free the emancipatory capacities of the oppressed and exploited lot of this world. Therefore, I must admit, it gives me a curious sensation to give a keynote speech, given such a strange background, since for me, keynote speeches have always meant two things: setting the tone of what is to be discussed, or exploring the possible breakthroughs that have emerged given the issues under discussion. Either way, it requires vivid clarity on the issues to do so. The latter is even more serious in that it requires one to avoid the pitfalls of going down well-trodden paths to try and emerge with new ideas.

Still, I have to give a keynote speech on the search of national and regional renewal in East Africa in the current conjecture. I have to interrogate the intellectual community. I have therefore decided to talk about The New Partnership for Africa's Development (NEPAD) as an intellectual 'product' of some of the African intellectuals, since this programme makes claims for the renewal and regeneration of Africa within attempts to unite Africa. My choice of NEPAD is a deliberate one, since it raises questions regarding the confluence of a lack of creativity and a loss of collective memory among many African leaders and intellectuals.

I plead for the indulgence of those who are already familiar with this Partnership and its criticisms. This is in recognition of the fact that over the past 30 years or so, there have also been other intellectuals, who despite all the odds, have continued questioning the crust of the post-independence privileges, raising questions that seek to transcend the existing arbitrary relationships, whether economic, social, political or cultural. These have been both reflecting upon and crystallising the woes and concerns of their people—those who are marginalized, exploited and oppressed. Recent years have produced many fundamental critiques of NEPAD from all over the continent—for example, those who participated in the African Social Forum in Bamako, Mali (January 2002) and CODESRIA together with the Third World Network-Africa in Accra, Ghana (April 2002) and many others. It is to these intellectuals who are concerned with the possibilities of transcending neo-liberalism that we must turn to, if we have to grasp the actual role of intellectuals in the search for renewal in Africa.

The 1980s and 1990s Intellectual Context

The late 1970s to early 1980s were years of theoretical and practical reaction. This was the period that saw the beginning of the implementation of International

Monetary Fund (IMF) and World Bank (WB) sponsored Structural Adjustment Programmes (SAPs), as a means to overcome the crisis that had begun to face many countries in Africa. According to the World Bank, Africa's stagnation was due to the following 'formal sector' policies: (1) political rather than economic criteria guiding investment choice, location and management; (2) regulations and wage controls that raised unit costs and undermined competitiveness; (3) high costs passed onto downstream users of outputs of heavily protected and inefficient basic industries; (4) expatriates (being)…removed before qualified nationals were available to take their place; and (5) private investment crowded out where the state controlled powerful monopolies.[1]

With such reasoning, the key issue became that of creating an 'enabling environment' for the efficient functioning of the private formal sector, through partly the improvement of infrastructure and the banking sector, but also mainly through state withdrawal from involvement in production and most services, deregulation of the conditions under which the private sector operated, and improved incentives for investments. With more foreign investments, it was claimed, benefits would trickle down to other sectors, including the informal one. According to the WB, transnational capital did not necessarily compete with local capital; rather it occupied a special place in that it complemented it. This was because it was the bearer of innovation, technical know-how and market intelligence. Other sectors would share this benefit.

SAPs had become the dominant discourse among many African intellectuals. They had also become the answer to welfarism and socialism, within the context of the salvation of the image of imperialism and capitalism in general. From the 1960s and 1970s traditions of the African intellectual community being involved —for better or for worse—in 'ideological struggles' and 'public debates' about 'development of underdevelopment', and how to transform and unify the neo-colonised African societies, it had become locked in the narrow short-term economism of the International Financial Institutions (IFIs) world view since the 1980s, blind to the real costs (human, material and psychological) in the short and the long run. The educated in Africa had become terribly short of ideals, and they had reached a position in which they 'listen very carefully to donors and researchers', as one study on SAREC's support showed.[2] This mainly followed the pattern of funding, where developmentalist research was rewarded and critical inquiry was refused. Donors were quite willing to reward work which confined itself to narrow problems—those that were functional to the state and not those involved in probing deeper.

Attempts to conceptualise the possibilities of how to build African societies organised in a humane way, devoid of inequalities and exploitation, became less fashionable from the 1980s. The new fashion manifested itself in terms of the organisation of seminars and conferences, conducted in hotels and conference centres, with restricted audience, 'sitting allowances', a marked presence of government officials and the virtual absence of the public. Discussions shifted to the question of the socio-economic crisis and means to overcome it, around the terms and conditions set out by the WB and the IMF. It was the economists who were in the front-line among the educated, but lacking in originality and openly endorsing the implementation of SAPs. These seminars and conferences were heavily funded, and the economists took upon themselves the task of advising the governments on the best ways to implement those policies.

Under these conditions, serious research and scholarship was increasingly marginalized, since according to the new pragmatic wisdom, to be reflective was not going to 'solve immediate problems'. The term 'academic' had turned into invective and to be an academic had become an aberration. What was becoming dominant was an instrumentalist view of scholarship and research—the view that research must serve particular political ends and the promotion of consultancies and their attendant Terms of Reference (TOR)—all serving short-range, narrow objectives to the exclusion of everything else.

Social scientists in general had become suppliers of recipes of the rationalisation of the practical or semi-theoretical of the worldviews of the dominant classes of this world. Many academics were increasingly living off academe, rather than for it. The universities were becoming ways of getting ahead in the world economically or politically. Their positions allowed them to vend their skills to the market of donors, NGOs and other funding institutions. What this amounted to is the fact that in practice, the world had reached a situation whereby the state no longer needed the services of the intellectuals for purposes of legitimation as it was once the case in history, since the upper classes had become capable of fiddling with statistics (that is computer technology for you!), while the middle class were busy bargaining in the market stock-exchange and the lower classes were made to await the fortunes from jackpot bingo or the choice of beauty pageants and now Big Brother Africa!

Many of the educated in Africa had become willing accomplices of the forces that worked against the emancipation of the people of Africa, hardly producing any solutions in thinking as far as the problems facing Africa are concerned. Many simply resigned to responding to the so-called 'globalising trends' and the need to be competitive internationally. Many educated Africans were increasingly pandering to the human predicament, rather than contributing to truly public and social interests (relevance and concern for human predicament). Within this context, the lack of historical consciousness or collective memory became the norm. Many intellectuals increasingly became ignorant of what was happening to their neighbouring countries due to the absence of regional, continental and even Pan-Africanist historicity. This was increasingly finding its expression in impatience with depth, shallowness in theories, art, literature, aesthetics, and so forth.

In this context, the ground for the internalisation of the conception that the world has become 'globalised' was laid. With this internalisation, the hitherto popular conceptions of global pillage were replaced by those of a global village. A new era had dawned: rather than the workers and peasants being the history movers, increasingly, it was rulers, ministers, investors, employers, expatriates and even local 'experts', legitimated by academic qualifications and the authority of science (especially economics), who became the agents of history, since it was them who knew better what is reasonable, modern and desirable change. The millions of the working people, peasant movements, trade unions and critical intellectuals were relegated to the position of unreason, stupidity and conservatism—people who did not understand the functioning of the 'new global system'.

SAPs ushered in an era pregnant with euphemisms. Thus neo-colonialism and imperialism became so-called 'globalisation' (globalise simply means global lies!). Exploiters were rehabilitated and became 'investors' or better still, 'the vital force of our nations'. It was no longer the alliance of the workers and peasants, but the 'partnership between the state, donors, private sector and NGOs'. A company or institution, which fired its workers, was said to be 'downsizing', 'retrenching' or 'slimming' (supposedly sport-like since a healthy body is supposed to be thin). And sacking workers was supposed to be a 'bold move', given the new economics, which dictated that either you 'compete or you go under'. Selling of public and national rights in the form of privatisation was re-labelled 'injecting sound economic policies': the introduction of 'flexibility' or 'deregulation'. The unemployed were said to be in the 'informal sector' or were 'self-employed'.

The world had entered an era in which consumer dominance, it was claimed, had become the new logic of society and not real societal needs, and individuals were being integrated into this consumer society through seduction or repression. This 'supermarket ideology' went as far as redefining 'love' in terms of the relationship between a person and his/her car, 'revolution' as a new brand of soap, a microwave oven or a washing machine, 'freedom/Uhuru' as possession of a cellular phone, 'democracy' as acceptance and tolerance of real differences by agreeing to disagree, 'partnership' (or so-called Smart Partnership!) as an exploitative relationship between man and woman, the poor and the rich, oppressor and oppressed, boss and worker, etc, 'participation' as acceptance of decisions from the powers that be under duress,[3] 'knowledge' and 'truth' as the power to cheat and deceive.

Those who were poor were so not because they were exploited, powerless, dominated, persecuted and marginalized, but because they were work-shy, and thus a problem for the rest of the society, since they could not budget, save and invest. It was claimed that, with globalisation, technology and economics had fused to the extent that human experience had become nothing more than a fictitious construct. The human subject had been belittled; instead, 'pluralism', 'multiplicity of differences' (so-called post-modernism) was the New Hope of these times. Vices were turned into virtues and the wicked and villains became heroes while the Masalakulangwa and Robin Hoods[4] of the world increasingly became objects of ridicule and cynicism.

Among numerous concepts that increasingly became fashionable among African intellectuals were terms such as 'globalisation', 'civil society', 'citizenship', 'good governance', 'multiparty democracy', 'poverty alleviation', 'Participatory Poverty Assessment', 'partnership in development', 'social safety nets', 'participatory development', 'informal sector', 'entrepreneurship', 'vulnerability', 'targeting the poor' and so on. These were popularised by the media, academia, international and regional financial institutions, advertisers, and publicists. They became the hallmark of the triumph of neo-liberalism and the New Right, couched in terms of the worldwide success of a 'free market economy' and 'liberal democracy' (globalisation).

Today, globalisation is presented as a system that offers 'opportunities and challenges'. It is proclaimed, There Is No Alternative (TINA—á la Margaret Thatcher, who went as far as declaring that there is no such a thing as society, but only individuals and families) since the world had reached the 'end of history' (á la Francis Fukuyama). Globalisation is presented in such a way that one is made to 'either adapt or perish', since there is no other future for the world. To take advantage of the opportunities, the world is told, important ingredients are things like 'individualism' and entrepreneurship, which would ensure that citizens have an unhampered freedom to pursue their interests (given the illusion of the unlimited possibilities of the 'informal sector' to make an entrepreneur of everybody who is 'resourceful'); 'human rights', which would safeguard the individual's property rights; 'good governance', which would establish the rule of law and take care of corruption; multiparty democracy and 'free and fair' elections, which would ensure that citizens exercise their right of choosing who should govern them; a vibrant 'civil society' with Non-Governmental Organisations (NGOs)—local and international flourishing without major hindrances; and an 'enabling environment' to attract funds from donors and investors.

New Economics of Plunder and Africa's Domination (NEPAD)

NEPAD is Africa's latest development initiative, after several initiatives in the past which on the whole were never implemented. It is a merger of the 'Millennium Action Plan for African Recovery Programme' (MAP), 'The Omega Plan' and 'The New Compact with Africa'. The buzz words in this initiative are globalisation and renaissance. These buzz words have become extremely popular in the past two decades or so. In my little recollection, it was the Jimmy Carter Centre which way back in 1987 or so, proclaimed that the next millennium would be the millennium of Africa's Renaissance. Renaissance, in the Centre's terms, was conceptualised in terms of economic regeneration.

Thabo Mbeki popularised the concept of 'African renaissance'. In his statement at the African renaissance Conference in Johannesburg in September 1998, he took cue from the Afrikaner youths who had declared that 'yesterday is a foreign country—tomorrow belongs to us!' For him, Renaissance was meant to 'address the critical question of sustainable development which impacts positively on the standard of living and the quality of life of the masses of our people'. It was a question of Africans inserting themselves into the 'international debate about the issue of globalisation and its impact on the lives of the people' and making their voice heard about what they and the rest of the world should do in order to 'achieve the development which is a fundamental right of the masses of our people'.

After consultation with some elites in 2000, during a meeting with Bill Clinton in May, the Okinawa G-8 meeting in July, the UN Millennium Summit in September, and subsequent European meetings in Portugal, Mbeki concretised his 'Millennium Africa Recovery Plan' as part of his vision of African Renaissance. It was produced with the assistance of economists and ratified 'during a special South African visit by World Bank president James Wolfensohn "at an undisclosed location", due presumably to fears of the disruptive protests which had soured a Johannesburg trip by new IMF czar, Horst Koehler a few months earlier'.[5] Thabo Mbeki recruited onto the bandwagon of this new vision of African Renaissance, presidents Abdelaziz Bouteflika from Algeria, Abdoulaye Wade from Senegal and Olusegun Obasanjo from Nigeria. This is the Plan that was to become the New Partnership for Africa's Development (NEPAD) in 2001. President Benjamin Mkapa was among those present at the World Economic Forum in Davos, when Thabo Mbeki presented this 'new vision' to the world's leading capitalists and state elites in early 2002.

NEPAD was popularised in all the leading industrial countries—Japan, Europe and USA. It was launched in Abuja, Nigeria by several African heads of state on 23 October 2001 after being endorsed by the meeting of the African Union in Lusaka, Zambia as a continental plan for Africa's economic regeneration as Africa's own initiative in July 2001. In February 2002, global elites celebrated NEPAD in sites ranging from the World Economic Forum meeting in New York City summit of self-described 'progressive' national leaders (but including the neo-liberal Tony Blair) who gathered in Stockholm to forge a global Third Way. All elite eyes were turning to the world's 'scar' (Blair's description of Africa), hoping that Nepad would serve as a large enough band aid.[6] The G8 endorsed NEPAD at Kananaskis through its Africa Action Plan, before being tabled at the launching of the African Union in July 2002 in Durban.

Without going into the details of the Programme itself, a critical examination of NEPAD leads one to conclude that those intellectuals who prepared the document behaved like Rip Van Winkle[7] as far as the historical experiences of Africa and the interrogation of the policies that have been advanced by the IFIs in the past 30 years or so to overcome underdevelopment were concerned. It is more or less the logic of the International Financial Institutions (IFIs), which is behind NEPAD's thinking. NEPAD placed nearly all the blames for Africa's problems and almost all the responsibility for sorting them out on Africa itself. Although it paid lip service to the fact that colonialism, the Cold War and the 'workings of the international economic system' had contributed to Africa's problems, it put the primary responsibility on 'corruption and economic mismanagement' at home. Nowhere did the document mention the more consequential corruption, mismanagement and exploitation by the powerful nations—to whom NEPAD sought to appeal. Those who prepared the document acknowledged that the underlying problem of the continent was debt. But they implicitly accepted the notions perpetuated by the rich nations that Africa has failed to progress because it had planned poorly in the past and had allowed rampant personal corruption.

Even the consequences of the domination of the Bretton Woods institutions and their policies were not taken to task at all. It appears that rather than denouncing them, they were only too anxious to embrace the Structural Adjustment Programmes. NEPAD pledged to support its successor policies and the Africa Growth and Opportunity Act (AGOA) passed by the US Congress. The document promised to eliminate poverty, enrol all children in primary school, reduce child mortality and supply clean water and infrastructure by means of 'public and private partnerships', a strategy whose performance has been very poor in the past twenty years or so. If the G8 endorsed NEPAD at Kananaskis, it is because it absolved these nations from all responsibility for the historic injustices meted out to the people of Africa.

The document fell short of even the initiatives of the World Conference Against Racism in Durban, South Africa, in September 2001, when 6000 delegates from 153 countries gathered to expose the evil of racism or the Gorée Conference that condemned slavery inflicted on Africa as a crime against humanity. No wonder that the document made very few references to human and people's rights, and even when these were made, it was in a rhetorical manner. Hardly did it also make any efforts to guarantee self-determination for the people, and in a way, it advanced policies that are incompatible with democracy and people's rights. It was not even critical of the fact that Overseas Development Aid (ODA), is used to impose economic and political conditionalities on the governments and peoples of Africa. Instead it took ODA as a basis for Africa's development. In this way, it accepted the fundamentals of the SAP paradigm by uncritically endorsing the so-called Poverty Reduction Strategy Programmes (PSPRs). The document could not discern that poverty reduction strategies that are being currently sponsored so heavily are part of the approach of 'pursuing Darwinist economics and then sending in Florence Nightingale to tidy up', which is a 'difficult and counterproductive approach to development'.[8]

The intellectuals who prepared this document seem to have completely forgotten that Africa rejected those global development strategies when it produced the Lagos Plan of Action, for example in 1980, a document that stood for 'collective self-reliance'. This document pointed out clearly that Africa 'remains the least developed continent... Africa is susceptible to the disastrous effects of natural and endemic diseases of the cruellest type and is victim of settler exploitation arising from colonialism, racism and apartheid. Indeed, Africa was directly exploited during the colonial period and for the past two decades, this exploitation has been carried out through neo-colonialist external forces which seek to influence the economic policies and directions of African States'.[9] The Abuja Treaty of 1981 had also rejected the neo-liberal wisdom of SAPs, and other documents that were to do the same were such as the African Alternative Framework to Structural Adjustment Programmes of 1989, the African Charter for Popular Participation and Development (the Arusha Charter) of 1990, and the Cairo Agenda of 1994.

Even the United Nations Economic Commission for Africa, had criticised the policies of the World Bank and International Monetary Fund in the 1980s. It accused the World Bank of selectivity and inconsistency, and of coming to misleading conclusions. As far as the Commission was concerned, the major weakness of SAPs was that they used short-term approaches to solve long-term problems. Such short-term stabilisation tended to divert attention from action, to attain sustainable longer-term economic growth and development goals. In some countries, according to the Commission, the undifferentiated sudden trade liberalisation (e.g. reduction of import tariffs) gave rise to the process of de-industrialisation. More serious was the fact that even those reform efforts had failed because of the vested interests of certain groups. The Commission showed that the trade-able goods sector opposed devaluation; firms producing import substitutes opposed trade liberalisation; farmers objected to doing away with agricultural subsidies; workers opposed privatisation and retrenchment; poor people detested cost-sharing as far as social services and infrastructure were concerned.[10]

Those intellectuals who prepared NEPAD took for granted that there was no alternative for the dominant thinking about how the world is - an inevitability of some sort. They took for granted that maximum growth, and therefore productivity and competitiveness, are the ultimate and sole goals of human action; or that economic forces cannot be resisted.[11] They accepted as inevitable, the irresponsibilisation of the state and the removal of the notion of the public and public interests, submitting the African people to the 'belief' of the values of the economy—the 'return of individualism' (self-help, self employment, cost-sharing, etc) and the destruction of all philosophical foundations of welfarism and collective responsibility towards poverty, misery, sickness, misfortunes, and education. These are the achievements which had been made by African intellectuals before the onslaught of SAPs, which have been thrown away on the pretext of 'reducing costs' of investors and creating an 'enabling environment' for them.

African Intellectuals and the Renewal of Africa

One thing that has become obvious in recent years is the fact that despite the rhetoric about democracy and freedom of expression, the use of excessive force against those who oppose globalisation has been on the increase. It is in this regard that one is compelled to ask questions such as: What is new about globalisation? Aren't the elements identifying it a mere re-labelling of what was termed colonialism/neo-colonialism or imperialism in the past? Aren't the elements identifying it the same as those that were claimed to be the features of a 'post-industrial society'? Given the debates surrounding the whole question of globalisation and its consequences, are there any quantitative or qualitative indicators to measure the degree of this process or lack of it?

Other questions can be asked: In which way, for example, can ordinary people realise what globalisation is, judging by their own standards, if they are not told about it, and given that what they face every day is reinforced marginalisation, hierarchisation and inequalities, the heightening of tensions and the deepening of immerseration—things which have existed in the history of capitalism? Why is it that some of the basic experiences have to be re-qualified, even if not rationally explained, as globalisation? Given that there is already ample evidence that globalisation in one way or another has been responsible for the erosion of people's welfare, job destruction and mass unemployment, and has thrown people into deeper immerseration and tensions, isn't the uncritical acceptance of globalisation an attempt to turn vices into virtues?

These questions are hardly posed by many of us in Africa. At the academic and popular level, the tyranny of globalisation and good governance in contemporary Africa invokes in the minds the image of the cursed old man of the sea whom Sinbad the Sailor found it impossible to shake off once he had allowed him to mount on his shoulders. Surprisingly, this is despite the fact that there have been anti-globalisation road shows in the world since the 1990s—first in Mexico in 1994 (with the peasants uprising against the North American Free Trade Agreement—NAFTA) and later on starting in 1999 in Seattle, until today. These road shows were an overt revolt against an open international economy in the advanced countries, in favour of protectionism from a broad political spectrum—environmentalists, trade unionists and many other civil activist organisations.

The Porto Alegre January–February meeting of 2001 (where more than 20,000 activists from all over the world gathered) and January–February 2002 (where more than 40,000 activists from all over the world met) for the World Social Forum, and the January 2002 and African Social Forum (in Bamako, where 250 activists from 43 countries gathered) meetings were the epitome of the revolts against 'globalisation'. The former declared that 'Another World is Possible', and the latter, 'Another Africa is Possible'.

In an attempt to answer the above questions practically, the anti-globalisation protestors have revealed that globalisation is a kind of politics, which has submitted governments and peoples to economic and social forces that are seemingly out of control. These are conscious and calculated politics of concentrated powers of big international concerns, such as the World Trade Organisation and multi-national networks.[12] The African Social Forum went as far as rejecting 'neo-liberal globalisation and further integration of Africa into an unjust system as a basis for its growth and development'. In this context, there was a "strong consensus that initiatives such as NEPAD (New Partnership for African Development), which are inspired by the IMF-WB strategies of Structural Adjustment Program-mes, trade liberalisation" that continue to subject Africa to an unequal exchange, and strictures on governance borrowed from the practices of Western countries are not rooted in the culture and history of the peoples of Africa."[13]

For those who were celebrating 'globalisation', these aspirations amounted to a midsummer night's dream. In Africa today, there are intellectuals who still believe in the mythologies of globalisation—a process that amounts to no more than an intellectual programme of desired goals, and not an analysis of what is actually taking place on the ground. That is, even when the end of an era is clearly perceived by people in other continents, the owls of Minerva (the goddess that symbolises knowledge) are still reluctant to take flight with twilight closing in. By uncritically swallowing and internalising the neo-liberal wisdom, they have become socially irresponsible intellectuals who are perpetuating abuse, prejudices, mediocrity, regressive and repressive interests wrapped in forms of 'universalism of the west'.

NEPAD claims its inspiration and legitimacy from the concept of the 'African Renaissance'. It has gone as far as producing misconceptions about what the African Renaissance is supposed to be. Generically, this 'new' conception of African Renaissance does not have any relation, say, with the past struggles of Africans to overcome injustices and transcend all forms of arbitrary relations, but with the global economic development strategies. That is, this renaissance has nothing to do with those traditions of the past that have always sought to stand against the destruction of all those ideals associated with public services, equality of rights, rights to education, health, culture, research and art. There is the absence of all the radical elements that have always been the hallmark of conceptions about African Renaissance—from Pan-Africanism, the Harlem Re-naissance, Negritude, African nationalism, and African Revolution in this con-ception of African Renaissance, since it has injected notions of globalisation which are morally rehabilitating imperialism.

If we will have to take seriously the call for an African Renaissance/Renewal, then the preconditions for it are the existence of a body of critical intellectuals, who are first and foremost capable of taking the immense responsibility of being competent, besides being a moral authority, fully committed to the politics of the radical witnesses—those who sleep with empty bellies and children who have never experienced childhood because they have to wield guns at a tender age. It is the existence of a community of intellectuals ready and capable of defending the ideals of social justice, and not those so-called abstract 'individual rights', which as we witness contemporarily, are ending up in the glorification of vices.

Such an intellectual body must of necessity avoid the unwitting pitfalls of demolition of 'metanarratives', as it is the fashion now, or the simple application and use of models. It must win the intellectual high ground for theoretical independence by attempting to deal with the question: What does it mean to be an African in a world whereby one's humanity is contested? In this case, it is necessary to take philosophy and philosophical debates seriously—as that 'discipline that has traditionally underwritten both what constitutes science or knowledge and which political practices are deemed legitimate'.[14] Such a community must be in a position to interrogate the various ontologies in the world, the kind of accounts of the world they give and their status in Africa. It is those emancipatory forms of knowledge, which should inform their practices—those forms of knowledge, which are oriented to human wellbeing (our mutual survival) and environmentally sustainable forms of life. Against all the cynicism of the morality established by Darwinism (the cult of the winner, the survivor), they must stand against the destruction of all those ideals associated with public services, equality of rights, rights to education, health, culture, research, and art. This is the basis of any meaningful Renaissance or even democratisation—the fulfilment of peoples' needs.

Champions of African Renaissance of the past include personalities such as Cheikh Anta Diop, Léopold Sédar Senghor, Aimé Césaire, Alioune Diop, Frantz Fanon and all the others; nationalists and revolutionaries such as Julius Nyerere, Kwame Nkrumah, Patrice Lumumba, Gamal Nasser and Amilcar Cabral; theoreticians such as Theophile Obenga, Eboussi Boulaga, M. Towa and Pauline Hountondji. These people tried to take up the challenge to equip theoretically the anti-imperialist resistance of the masses of the African people. It was this resistance that expressed the real essence of African Renaissance. The same needs to be the central issue today.

Any meaningful Renaissance in Africa must be linked to those past struggles. The past cannot be a foreign country, since it still haunts the present. Historical experiences and practices, which made possible the emergence and transformation of ideological positions for, or against the transformation of Africa are important to be taken aboard. It is with the examination of the strengths and weaknesses of the rebelling masses in the past and the present by committed intellectuals, and the search for ways of equipping them as history makers, within a specific historical moment and social milieu (class, gender, caste or race specific), that they will be able to play a meaningful role. They must strive to work for building a future that has no place for one's humanity being contested.

Like Issa Shivji who ended his speech with a poem, I wish to do the same. It is from our sister Micere Githae Mugo:

Tell me

tell me whether

their theories are

active volcanoes

erupting with fertilizing lava

on which to plant

seeds that will

germinate

with self-knowledge

seeds that will

cross-fertilize

into collective being

Knowledge become

action theory

Knowledge become

living testimony

of our people's

affirmative history

liberated herstory

Actioned theory

inscribed as protest

manifesto

re-aligning our people's

averted humanity

Yes, tell me this

and I will tell you

whether they are

intellectuals

or imposters.[15]

Notes

* This paper was presented as a Keynote Speech for the East Africa Sub-Regional Conference, 'East Africa: In Search of National and Regional Renewal'. More or less the same ideas were presented in the International Conference on 'The Role of the Educated Class in Africa: Between African Renaissance and Globalisation— A Critique', 21-23 March 2003, at Evangelische Akademie Loccum, Rehburg-Loccum, Germany; and during the commemoration of Africa Day organised by Dar es Salaam University Political Science Association in collaboration with Pan African Youth Movement (Tanzania Chapter), at the University of Dar es Salaam on 25th May 2003. The paper is based on a reworking of various ideas that I have presented before.

1. World Bank, *Sub-Saharan Africa: From Crisis to Sustainable Growth*, World Bank, Washington DC, 1989, pp. 110–11.

2. C. Widstrand, *Tanzania: Development of Scientific Research and Sarec's Support 1977– 1991*, SAREC Documentation, Stockholm, 1992. p. 23.

3. The most cynical type of participation, which in a way reveals so much about the modern political gimmicks is karaoke—the 'vox pox' participatory performance art, where one is invited to sing a song by Jim Reeves, Dolly Parton, Michael Jackson, etc. Here anybody, it is claimed, can be whoever he/she wants to imitate!

4. Masalakulagwa is a character in the Wasukuma oral literature. He is a hero who fought against ghouls or goblins that gobbled up people. Robin Hood is a legendary figure, supposed to have lived at a time when laws were unfair and the poor were left to starve, who used to rob the rich and the noblemen and gave to the poor. The metaphor is from Ann McGovern's Robin Hood of Sherwood Forest (Scholastic Inc, New York, 1968).

5. For details, see Patrick Bond (ed.), *Fanon's Warning: A Civil Society Reader on the New Partnership for Africa's Development*, African World Press, Inc, Trento, New Jersey, 2002, p. 8.

6. Ibid, p. 9.

7. Rip Van Winkle is a hero in a story under the same title by Washington Irving. Van Winkle drank liquor in strange company, and fell asleep and did not awake for twenty years!

8. Jan Nederveen Pieterse, 'Equity and Growth Revisited: A Supply-Side Approach to Development', *European Journal For Development Research*, No 4, 1997.

9. Organisation of African Unity, Lagos Plan of Action, 1980, p. 5.

10. See D. Reed, *Structural Adjustment and the Environment*, Earthscan Publications, London, 1992.

11. Pierre Bourdieu, *Acts of Resistance: Against the New Myths of our Time*, Polity Press, Cambridge, 1998, p. 30.

12. The delegates to this first-ever World Social Forum, a global gathering of trade unions, social movements, non-governmental organizations (NGOs) and progressive-minded intellectuals (about 144 organisations) produced a document which appealed to the people of the world to fight 'the hegemony of finance, the destruction of our cultures, the monopolization of knowledge and of the mass communications media, the degradation of nature and the destruction of quality

of life'. According to the document, these actions are carried out 'by transnational corporations and anti-democratic policies'.

13. African Social Forum, 'The Bamako Declaration/Statement: Another Africa Is Possible!'.

14. Roy Bhaskar, *Reclaiming Reality: A Critical Introduction to Contemporary Philosophy*, Verso, London, 1989, p 1.

15. Micere Githae Mugo, 'Intellectuals or impostors?', *My Mother's Poems and Other Songs*, East African Educational Publishers, Nairobi, 1994, p. 28.

References

Bhaskar, R., 1989, *Reclaiming Reality: A Critical Introduction to Contemporary Philosophy*, Verso, London, pp 1.

Bond, P., ed., 2002, *Fanon's Warning: A Civil Society Reader on the New Partnership for Africa's Development*, African World Press, Inc, Trento, New Jersey, pp. 8.

Bourdieu, P., 1998, *Acts of Resistance: Against the New Myths of our Time*, Polity Press, Cambridge, pp. 30.

McGovern, A., 1968, *Robin Hood of Sherwood Forest* (Scholastic Inc, New York).

Mugo, M.G., 1994, 'Intellectuals or impostors?', *My Mother's Poems and Other Songs*, East African Educational Publishers, Nairobi, pp. 28.

Nederveen Pieterse, J., 1997, 'Equity and Growth Revisited: A Supply-Side Approach to Development', *European Journal for Development Research*, No 4.

Organisation of African Unity, 1980, Lagos Plan of Action, pp. 5.

Reed, D., 1992, *Structural Adjustment and the Environment*, Earthscan Publications, London.

World Bank, 1989, *Sub-Saharan Africa: From Crisis to Sustainable Growth*, World Bank, Washington DC, pp. 110-11.

Widstrand, C., 1992, *Tanzania: Development of Scientific Research and Sarec's Support 1977–1991*, SAREC Documentation, Stockholm, pp. 23.

3

Language and Regional Integration: Foreign or African Languages for the African Union?

Sangai Mohochi

Introduction

True to the Kiswahili adage that 'umoja ni nguvu' (unity is strength), it has become fashionable to seek strength in unity. This is evident, for instance, in the corporate world where different organisations are seeking mergers in order to face the ever-increasing challenges in business. The same has become true of nations in most parts of the world. They realise that it is very difficult for most of them to face the international world single-handedly. The developing nations, which have weak economies, need integration much more than the more developed nations, but unfortunately, it is the latter that have moved faster to reap the advantages of regional integration.

Africa is home to many of the very poor people in the world. As such, African leaders have a duty to take bold steps in an attempt to try and uplift the living standards of their people. This can be reached much faster not by relying on foreign aid that is more often than not pegged to very difficult conditions, but rather by striving together. There is an abundance of natural resources on the continent that require to be exploited for faster growth and economic development. This however cannot be reached unless the climate is conducive, and one way in which such a climate can be attained is by stronger and functional regional integration.

Regional Integration

Due to globalisation and increased liberalisation, there is a massive increase in levels of interdependence amongst nations. The increasing volume of cross-border trade has resulted in consumers even in the remotest of places, gaining access to a wider variety of goods and services than hitherto. However, in order to be able to participate in such an arrangement, nations must be able to articulate their needs and aspirations in international trade agreements with a strong voice.

On our ability to bargain, Ndegwa (1986:106) notes: 'Because of their economic and therefore political weaknesses, African countries have sometimes not been taken seriously internationally in global discussions or in bilateral dealings with large developed countries'. Unfortunately, that is the truth and indeed, we can not command the much needed respect and bargaining ability individually as Kenyans, Nigerians, Liberians and so on. But if united, we shall command considerable bargaining power. Therefore, in order to benefit from the prevailing and future world trade arrangements, African countries urgently need to work together.

Ng'andu (1998:2) states that in recognition of the fact that many ACP countries were in the category of least developed countries, the WTO trade regime granted a waiver to the Lome Convention under which 47 African, 15 Caribbean and 8 Pacific countries were to have trade preferences with 15 members of the European Union. It was felt that these countries needed a transition during which they would continue to enjoy preferential trading arrangements. The question that remains unanswered is whether African countries have really benefited much from these arrangements. Rather than wait for waivers, we must move faster to seek our own lasting solutions to the numerous problems facing us. This urgent need to work together is further elaborated by Ndegwa (1986:106), who reminds us that '... African countries should also be aware of the decreasing amount of real foreign assistance from those developed countries and the widening and deepening protectionism the developed countries are practicing against imports from the poor countries'. In view of the changing circumstances, the above-mentioned waivers are no longer guaranteed. These are harsh realities, which should serve to ignite the spark of cooperation among all Africans, including the many sceptics.

There are certain necessary ingredients that help attract both domestic and foreign investment, and since investment is a necessary component of trade, we need to attract as many investors as possible. However, apart from economic reforms that are meant to make trade easier, it is also essential to ensure that other infrastructure is in place. For instance, the size of the market is quite critical. Because of the poor physical infrastructure, dependence on primary commodities and a relatively small market size, it is very difficult for African countries to attract the much-needed foreign investment. Most African countries are small in terms of population. This calls for the need for an enlargement of the development base through intra-African trade in order to benefit from economies of scale in operating major services (Ndegwa 1986:111). Consequently, smaller regional blocs like the EAC, ECOWAS, SADC, though better than individual countries, are hardly enough. These are good starting points, but it is now time we started moving towards larger blocs.

It is indeed true that globalisation and liberalisation are the key words in the international discourse on growth and development, but at the same time there is a growing realisation of the need for closer regional ties. As Ndegwa (1986:122-123) puts it: 'indeed, some commentators argue that sub-regional groupings might at first be more economically and politically attainable and serve as building-blocks towards a continental unification based on them'. Many have gone beyond the realisation stage and actualised those desires where hitherto no ties existed, or have strengthened the existing ones. Ng'andu (1998:4) indicates that in the last twelve years, there has been an increase in the creation of regional economic and trading blocs. They have increased from about 20 to nearly 100. They are probably much more by now. The well known ones include: ASEAN in Asia, NAFTA in America, MERCUSOR in South America, the European Union, ECOWAS in West Africa, COMESA and SADC in Eastern and Southern Africa, the Pacific FORUM, and the CARIFORUM in the Caribbean.

In Central America, there have been numerous attempts at reviving the Central American Federation that was dissolved in 1838. Towards this end, 1963 saw the setting up of the Central American Common Market (CACM) that was unfortunately dissolved later. The System for Integration in Central America (SICA) was established in 1991 to take care of political and economic cooperation.

In many instances, economic development is an important driving force behind efforts at integration in different regions. The following is noted about Central America in this regard. 'First and foremost, Central America stands united in a bid to meet the challenges posed by the globalisation of economy and trade, including the formation of WTO. The formation of regional markets has become a widespread way of handling this development' (Publications in English, 2001:2). However, small regional groupings stand very little chance in world trade where larger groups call the shots. For its part, Central America has set out to establish closer ties with the North Atlantic Free Trade Area (NAFTA) mainly as a bridge to joining the Inter-American Free Trade Area (IAFTA) in the year 2005. This is largely because the North American Market is 200 times larger. The Central American countries' markets and production potential are very small and they must work together for better bargaining power. Indeed the same should apply to all smaller regional blocs. This is particularly true and significant in Africa. Africa, with the poorest nations, has very few such blocs and those in existence do not have the necessary muscle in the international arena. Ng'andu (1998:5) rightly puts it this way:

> For many African countries with serious capacity limitations, effective participation in the global economy is not possible. Sometimes, the rules of the game are so complex as to be understood only by the few trade officials and traders. As a way of capacity

enhancement, cooperation with neighbours on regional basis is the most viable option for integration into the global economy.

Regional Integration in Africa

Efforts at attaining integration in Africa are not new. They date back to the Pan-Africanism movement times, which played a crucial role in laying the ground for African integration. Whereas Black Americans from USA and the Caribbean dominated the Pan-African movement in the late 19th and 20th century, leaders from Africa began playing a greater role from the mid 20th century. Between 1900 and 1945, six Pan-African Congresses were held in different European cities. The last one, held in Manchester in 1945, was convened by the Pan-African Federation that had been formed in 1944, and was made up of 13 organisations representing students' welfare and political groupings under George Padmore, C.L.R. Wallace Johnson and Jomo Kenyatta. One pronouncement that came out of this congress is worth repeating: 'The congress also expressed the hope that before long, the peoples of Asia and Africa would have broken their chains of colonialism. Then, as free nations, they would stand united to consolidate and safeguard their liberties and independence from neo-colonialism' (K.I.E. 1986).

I believe that while expressing that optimism, Du Bois (West Indies); Jomo Kenyatta (Kenya); Kwame Nkrumah (Ghana); George Padmore (Trinidad); Peter Abrahams (South Africa); Otto Mackonnel (West Africa), and Magnus Williams representing Nnamdi Azikiwe (Nigeria), sincerely hoped for better living standards for the entire black race. While it is true that we are free nations as envisaged, in Africa we have neither managed to stand united nor have we been able to adequately speak with one voice against all new forms of exploitation. Subsequent African leaders stand accused of failure to follow the visionary leaders of the struggle for the liberation of Africa. Indeed as we shall point out shortly, our continued reliance on foreign languages is one way of perpetuating the neo-colonialism that these leaders spoke out against.

From as early as the late 1950s, Dr. Kwame Nkrumah preached the need for Africa to be united in order to be less vulnerable to outside influence. Nkrumah and other African leaders argued that 'Africa's political independence and the dignity of its people could not be fully achieved and protected without a 'United States of Africa' (Ndegwa 1986:111-112). That was no easy task. Discussions had been initiated to form an African organisation, but there emerged two opposing camps. There was the Casablanca group, which wanted immediate unity plans, and the Monrovia group that favoured a gradual approach. Finally, in May 1963, leaders of the then 32 independent African states met in Addis Ababa and signed a charter, establishing the Organisation of African Unity. Among the many areas of major concern were cooperation in areas of economy and social welfare, education and culture, and collective defence, as well as the possible establishment of regional economic groups. For quite some time, the OAU successfully served as an umbrella body that helped Africans find solutions to their problems. The political federation envisaged never materialised, but those efforts led to the formation of the OAU. However, along the line, probably due to a decline in the Pan-African spirit, the OAU became less and less effective and as a result there is urgent need to rethink the whole process of African unity.

There have been numerous cooperation arrangements both regionally as well as continentally. The earlier attempts, which Ravenhill (1985) refers to as the failed attempts at regionalism include the East African Community (EAC); the West African Customs Union (UDAO); the Central African Federation; the Economic and Customs Union of Central Africa, and the Mali Federation (Ndegwa 1986; Ravenhill 1985). Later regional blocs include the Preferential Trade Area (PTA); the Economic Community of West African States (ECOWAS), and the Southern African Development Coordination Conference (SADCC). Those already in existence need to be strengthened without undermining the newly launched African Union, since the two are meant to play complementary roles in Africa's development endeavours.

In an interview with *Suddeutsche Zeitung* (SZ), a Munich-based daily newspaper the then German foreign minister, Klaus Kinkel pleaded for regionalisation in Africa. Speaking about the OAU, he said; 'This large regional organisation with a membership of 53 countries, should take over a considerably larger responsibility for Africa than it has done until now. And we should help it in doing that'. The need for integration has finally dawned on many people the world over. Africans too have accepted it as an inevitable path to development and success. Speaking to students and staff of Egerton University in Kenya in January 2002, the Tanzanian prime minister, Frederick Sumaye (an alumnus of the institution) stressed the need for closer regional ties. He particularly pleaded with East Africans to take the new East African Community more seriously with a view to forming a political federation in the near future.

Despite all that has happened with regard to integration in Africa, there are those who believe that meaningful cooperation is not attainable on this continent. Ravenhill (1985), who seems to rule out any possibility of success of regionalism in Africa, is one such person. He asserts:

Africa, in fact, is uniquely ill suited for regional integration; at least, for the form most typically adopted by developing countries: the integration of markets... African economies, far from complementing each other, compete in the world market as exporters of primary products. But, more important, African economies are simply irrelevant to the needs of their neighbours – a problem compounded by the lack of physical infrastructure, which hampers communication. Add to this a variety of languages, currency areas, continuing close ties to ex-metropoles, and a critical shortage of skilled personnel, and one arrives at a very dismal scenario indeed (Ravenhill 1985:207).

While it is true that our infrastructure is largely poor and we still maintain ties with our ex-metropoles, the rest of what Ravenhill says is not entirely true. There is a great deal of trade among African economies. Neither do we simply compete as exporters of primary products in the world market. Africa, most certainly, has a wide pool of relevant and skilled personnel. As for languages, we have regional languages that can ably take care of our multilingualism. We do not face the hopeless and dismal scenario suggested by Ravenhill.

Indeed, there are many challenges to integration in Africa but then we must face up to them as best as we can. We simply cannot afford to do otherwise. The concerns of Africa and Africans are primarily our own business. We need to take the necessary steps rather than continue deceiving ourselves that foreign intervention of whatever form will solve the many economic and social problems that we are faced with. As is rightly pointed out by Ndegwa (1986), the solutions to our problems can only come through strategies based on collective self-reliance. Ravenhill (1985) also argues that we need to develop a basis of cooperation that takes into account our unique circumstances.

Language in Regional Integration

The World Bank has pointed out that in today's economically integrated world, trade matters more than ever before, and that there is compelling evidence that openness to trade is associated with increased growth (WB 2001). Openness to trade necessarily entails talking with our neighbours to draw up development strategies. How then does the question of language fit in this scenario? Quite naturally we must be able to communicate effectively in order to plan and forge ahead together in whatever integration arrangement we put in place. Without effective communication, we cannot talk about integration that involves the majority and goes beyond the meetings held by leaders at the never-ending summits.

Among the most important pillars of a strategy for successful cooperation that have been espoused by Ndegwa (1986) is education for the people on the need to cooperate, and public acceptance of the need to cooperate. In all of these, language is very important. There must be an effective communication system to rally the people behind whatever integration endeavours are being made. This will only be achieved if we resort to the use of a language(s) that is easily accessible to the majority. One problem cited as having been an impediment to plans for a political union in Central America is the failure to harness popular grassroots support for the integration process. The situation is explained as follows:

> ... the integration process – particularly plans for union – has largely been driven by elitist forces. The decision to form a political union has been taken centrally, with little conferring with civil societies, let alone national parliaments. Moves are also afoot to initiate a rapid process for creating

the union, and there is consequently a great risk, that union endeavours will not achieve any genuine popular anchorage (Publications in English, 2001:2).

A similar risk faces various regional groups in Africa, and would also trouble the African Union. We must endeavour to involve our people in whatever agreements we reach, and the only sure way to do so is through civic education. The public needs to feel that various decisions of the leaders are taken on their behalf, and to know how such decisions will impact on their lives. I know no better way to achieve this than using the rich repertoire of our languages to pass the message across. Unfortunately, most of our African governments are repelled by the mere mention of the term "civic education". By insisting on English and other foreign languages as we are doing now, we are only succeeding in shutting out about 80 percent of our population from popular participation in the development process.

Development and good governance are important national agendas in many countries. These should be given similar treatment in regional initiatives since there should be as much commonality of policies as possible among member states. Unfortunately, the linguistic means to achieving these goals are usually treated most casually. Okombo, in Ndambuki (2001:1), observes that the role of languages in achieving those goals is ignored in Kenya. This is true of almost all countries in Africa, and the situation needs to be addressed very urgently. The African Union is one body well suited to come up with a solution to the issue.

Okombo further argues that for development to occur, the African masses must be involved through the recognition of indigenous languages. Whatever policies we come up with must take cognisance of the plural character of Africa if they are to be of any use to Africa and her people. Multilingualism in Africa should be treated as a resource rather than a problem. While accepting Okombo's contentions, I hasten to add that the whole situation must be handled with great care. We cannot afford to accept all sorts of suggestions on the language issue in Africa simply because each group wants its language to play a role. This was clearly the case in Zambia in 2001, during the AU meeting, where Guinea, through its head of state, proposed the adoption of Spanish as one of the working languages of the Union. There will be a state of confusion in the African body if we were to accept all languages of the former colonisers. What reason shall we have to deny Portuguese if we accept Spanish? Probably we need to be driven by an assessment of the language use demands in Africa against the available language resources while making decisions on language matters. What direction should we take then with regard to the issue of language in the African Union?

Language, African Unity and Development

Language has been noted to be a very significant ingredient in unity. Consequently, on attainment of independence, most African states were faced with the need to choose a language through which national unity could be forged. Most chose the languages of their colonial masters as official and even national languages. These decisions were not easily reached since a number of people opposed them on the grounds that they perpetuated the colonial mentality. However, such decisions were explained on the ground that with the multiplicity of languages within their borders, it would have been difficult to choose one local language and not another. That was the general trend in Africa apart from a few exceptions like Tanzania and Kenya, which had an already widespread and accepted alternative in Kiswahili.

As it is now in Africa, all important national and international issues are discussed and decided in foreign languages. Since Africa was not colonised by a single European power, it follows that Africa is regionalised linguistically as each country maintains links with its coloniser, among other things, by maintaining the use of the coloniser's language. Consequently, we have French-, English- and Portuguese-speaking Africa. We often hear about either Anglophone or Franco-phone African leaders summits. Africa is therefore very divided linguistically with regard to foreign languages, and a decision to use one at the expense of the other is not possible. That is precisely why we have always had the idea of working languages of important bodies like the OAU, to cater for the different interests.

The situation is even worse with regard to indigenous languages. Africa is known to be extremely multilingual. There are many languages spoken in virtually all African states. Despite all that, it still remains a fact that the trend the world over, is to form regional groups and language is indeed an important part of this tendency. Given that situation, which language would best serve in fostering African unity? It has been estimated, for example, that only 5 percent of Nigeria's population are able to use English. Igue and Noueni (1994) describe a similar situation in Benin (Hansford 1994:76). The percentages might be different but the general trend in Africa is the same with regard to English and all other foreign languages.

Speaking about Benin, Igue and Noueni (1994:59) have captured a true picture of the whole of Africa on this issue. Our leaders at independence and all subsequent regimes have maintained the colonial language policies, hence imposing French, English or Portuguese on their citizens in most domains. As these authors note, '... This option has had grave consequences for the ability and willingness of the various populations to participate in the process of national, social, cultural and economic development'.

This has led to the rather unfortunate situation in which our populations are clearly segregated. On the one hand are the minority who have a mastery of the foreign language, and on the other, are the majority who speak one or more of the indigenous languages. As a consequence, those who can speak, read and write these 'superior' foreign languages have acquired undue advantage in accessing knowledge, money, power and status.

... In this way, the majority of the people do not participate in the push towards development since they are not able to be integrated into the communication process that is fundamental to the economic, social, political and cultural structures of the modern state... It is also evident that development can never occur when the great majority are marginalized by the use of a language, which simply allows an elite to conduct a monologue with itself (Igue & Noueni 1994:60).

As mentioned earlier, one of the major problems that have faced attempts at unity and integration in South America was lack of popular grassroots support. Most of our initiatives also lack mass support because the majority are basically marginalized. Continued insistence on the use of foreign languages only serves to marginalize our people. If integration in Africa is meant to bring positive development and change for the majority, we have no alternative but to turn to our languages as a means to achieving whatever goals we envisage. Fardon and Furniss (1994:85) comment that: 'At the same time, economic and technological development, if it is to involve the majority of the people, can be promoted only through the use of African languages'.

There is no better way of putting it, and I believe there is no way that we can attain any meaningful development through integration by relying on foreign languages. Bamgbose sums it as follows:

More recently it is becoming evident that the choice of an ex-colonial language for the purpose of national integration makes possible only horizontal integration. This involves the combination of the educated elites from the various linguistic groups, which may comprise only 10–15 percent of the population. The alternative, vertical integration would enable the integration of elites with masses and allow the vast majority of the people who have no access to the official languages to participate in the social, economic and political system. This sort of integration is only possible through an African language (quoted in Benjamin 1994:102).

According to Benjamin (1994:104), the liberation movement in South Africa, particularly in the 1930s and 1940s, advocated the use of English as a lingua franca since it would cut across ethnic divisions. Indeed similar arguments were advanced in other African countries in support of the ex-colonial languages. That argument holds no water any longer because we have African languages, which cut across ethnic divisions. These include Kiswahili, Hausa, Akan, Fulfulde and others. Maake (1994:119) observes that research in the trade union movement in South Africa has shown that the only way to be able to communicate with the majority of the workers is through African languages. That fact is neither confined to the trade union movement nor to South Africa. It is true for all spheres of life in Africa as a whole.

African Languages for the African Union

The development of African languages is not only necessary for national integration but for regional integration too. However, even after settling for African languages, there remains the problem of which language(s) should be used in the face of Africa's linguistic diversity. It is estimated that there are 2000 languages in Africa (Elugbe 1994, quoted in Fardon & Furniss 1994:62). This multiplicity of languages makes the language question a difficult issue. Indeed the question of the language best suited for African unity is one that has quite a long history. It has been a subject of concern to a number of scholars and other prominent sons of Africa. According to Benjamin (1994:102), as early as the 1940s, resentment existed towards language policies in Africa. When it emerged that the language policy in South Africa favoured Afrikaans and English at the expense of African languages, a view emerged within the Communist Party, with the support of the influential Soviet Africanist Prof. I. Potkin that called for the development of all African languages. However, within the liberation movement, there were Pan-Africanists who instead supported Swahili as a lingua franca. These were the earlier stages of a long-standing attempt to advance Kiswahili as a forerunner for the position of an African lingua franca. Many more people have advocated its choice.

Chimerah (1998), Okwany (1995), Mukama (1992) and Mazrui (1995) say that Swahili is no longer an East African language. It has diffused widely and is used in different parts of the world, particularly in the media and in educational institutions. Mazrui and Mazrui (1995) go a step further and state that Swahili is the most international of all African languages. Indeed it is the only linguistic export from Africa that has been widely accepted. Concerning what makes a world language, Ohly (1977:119) suggests that such a language should be able to meet the communication needs of various international organisations. Other important requirements include a wide distribution of speakers in different parts of the world, and a significant number of speakers. These are the factors that contributed to the development of English, French, Russian, Chinese, Spanish, and Arabic as world languages.

Among all languages of African origin, Swahili is the only language with a clear chance of emerging as a world language. It is spoken in varying degrees in Europe, America, Asia and Africa. According to Okwany (1995), there are well over 50 million speakers. Indakwa (1978) observes that the more than 50 million speakers do not in fact include speakers outside Africa. Swahili is the second language in Africa behind Arabic in terms of the number of speakers and the first among 86 Bantu languages (Ohly 1977). Swahili is therefore ahead of other African languages in many respects.

In the Second Congress of Black Writers and Artists in 1958, the issue of an African lingua franca was discussed at length. A decision to choose one language for that purpose was reached. Out of the discussions, Kiswahili, Hausa, Mande, Yoruba, Fulfilde, and Wolof were proposed (Indakwa 1978). And in The Second World Black and African Festival of Arts and Culture, held in Lagos Nigeria in 1976, renowned scholars Professors Wole Soyinka and Mohamed Abdulaziz threw their support behind the choice of Swahili as Africa's language. The Inter-African Bureau of Languages, which is an Organisation of African Unity organ, while advocating for wider usage of African languages, recommended Swahili, Hausa, Arabic, Lingala, and Zulu as languages for regional and continental contact (Phillipson and Skutnabb-Kangas 1995). Overall, there is more support for Swahili in comparison with the other suggested languages, mainly because of the following reasons:

i) It has proved its unifying ability by enabling effective communication between East Africans who speak English and their French-speaking neighbours of Central Africa.

ii) It has more speakers than all the other languages that have been suggested as an African lingua franca.

iii) It is a language that has a long written history with many publications on culture and literature.

iv) Swahili is a Bantu language that can be easily acquired in Africa as approximately half of Africa's population is made up of Bantu language-speakers whose languages are very closely related.

v) Kiswahili has proved to be flexible in its lexicon expansion. This makes it suitable for communication in a world that is continuously experiencing rapid changes scientifically, technologically and socially.

While noting that there are many other important African languages, Bamgbose (1994:34) also indicates the fact that Swahili has an edge over the others. 'Because of the utility of languages like Akan in Ghana, Wolof in Senegal, Hausa in northern Nigeria, Lingala in Zaire, *not to mention the more widely spoken Swahili in Eastern Africa*, speakers of different languages are embracing them as second languages' (our emphasis). Despite that realisation of Swahili's wide reach, Bamgbose (1994:36) elewhere, has attacked Soyinka's support for Kiswahili on the grounds that its development would make it a supra-national language. Again, due to the multiplicity of languages in Africa, Kiswahili has very many opponents. Most who are opposed to its elevation, hasten to point to its Arabic influence as a weakness, and insist that it should not serve as a lingua franca in Africa since it is as alien as English, French, and all the others.

Africa's multilingualism has occupied very many observers for quite some time. These include Bamgbose (1994), Benjamin (1994), Okombo (in Ndambuki,

2001), and Fardon and Furniss (1994). They point out the fact that multilingualism in Africa is seen as a source of problems and an impediment to development. Need that be the position? Do we not have very well known advantages in multilingualism? If we do, why cannot we look at the positive side, and work to lessen the negative impact? It has been pointed out, for instance, that there is governmental and academic unease with multilingualism in Africa (Fardon & Furniss 1994). Cannot we learn from countries that have managed their multilingual situations effectively like Canada (English & French), as well as Switzerland (French, German and Italian)? We need to develop and encourage multilingualism in Africa by taking note of the significance of both our own indigenous languages and the foreign languages as well. Citing Kashoki, Bamgbose (1994:34) insists that multilingualism is not a barrier to national unity and integration; and that a more integrated person is in fact one who is at ease with the several languages that are found in any African country. As much as we are advocating Swahili, we are aware that all other African languages are important. However, it would not be very easy to develop all of them equally for African Unity. We must also not lose sight of the significant role played by foreign languages. What we therefore need to do is to encourage our people to have a more extensive language repertoire. Bamgbose (1994:42) has argued:

> The conclusion, which seems inevitable in the situation of most developing countries, is that a multilingual policy is the only viable avenue for development. African languages will have well-defined roles in education, culture and mass communication without prejudice to the complementary role of LWCS – Languages of Wider Communication. Foreign ideas, concepts and technology will undoubtedly be imported in a foreign language, but such concepts must be transmitted to the masses in a language that they can understand. The economic miracle achieved by countries such as Japan is not based on a widespread dissemination of English; rather it is a result of the domestication of foreign technology in Japanese, and the translation of the productive processes into terms that the ordinary factory hand can understand.

The truth is that in Africa, multilingualism is largely unavoidable and we are better off developing it rather than fighting it. Fardon & Furniss (1994) have said that multilingualism is actually Africa's lingua franca. We must accept it and try to make it a resource through which our development goals can be attained. Katupha (1994:95) too takes note of our many languages and proposes functional bilingualism as a possible compromise between the preservation of our traditions and modernisation. Following on his suggestion, I would like to propose functional multilingualism instead. We need to develop local languages since everyone has linguistic human rights to enjoy in life: regional languages (lingua francas) for wider communication beyond our communities; Swahili for long-term wider communication in the African Union, and the European and other foreign languages for international interaction.

Conclusion

In the paper, we have indicated the ever-increasing need for integration for effective participation in a global world. Indeed there are attempts at creating regional groups in various parts of the world and strengthening the already existing ones. For Africa, due to our poor economies, there is a more urgent need to come together in the spirit of integration. As much as we have regional groups in Africa, we must work to strengthen the African Union, which can best bring together those many groups for the benefit of all. However, Africa has a unique problem stemming from its multilingual situation and the fact that there are a number of ex-colonial languages competing for supremacy in the continent. Since these foreign languages are familiar only to a very insignificant few, the only way of bringing as many Africans to own our development initiatives is by a shift in language policy. We must develop our languages for effective communication with the masses. We have proposed Swahili as the language best suited for development as a language for the African union. If that is not easy to attain in the short term, we can develop a number of African languages initially. Towards this end we suggest Hausa for West Africa, Arabic in the north, Zulu in South Africa, Swahili in East and Central Africa while encouraging the continued development of Kiswahili. If for valid reasons Swahili is not acceptable, I would vote for any other language as long as it is an indigenous African one.

References

Bamgbose, A., 1994, 'Pride and Prejudice in Multilingualism', in R. Fardon and G. Furniss (eds.) *African Languages, Development and the State*, London and New York: Routledge, pp. 33-43.

Benjamin, J., 1994, 'Language and the Struggle for Racial Equality in the Development of a Non-racial Southern African Nation', in R. Fardon and G. Furniss (eds.) *African Languages, Development and the State*, London and New York: Routledge, pp.97-110.

Chimerah, R., 1998, *Kiswahili Past, Present and Future Horizons*, Nairobi: Nairobi University Press.

Fardon, R. and Furniss, G., 1994, eds., *African Languages, Development and the State*, London and New York: Routledge.

Hansford, G.F., 1994, 'Using Existing Structures, Three phases of Mother Tongue Literacy Among Chumburung Speakers in Ghana', in R. Fardon and G. Furniss (eds.) *African Languages, Development and the State,* London and New York: Routledge, pp. 76-84.

Igue, M.A. and Noueni, R.W., 1994, 'The Politics of Language in Benin', in R. Fardon and G. Furniss (eds.) *African Languages, Development and the State*, London and New York: Routledge, pp. 55-61.

Indakwa, J., 1978, 'A "Lingua Franca" for Africa', *Kiswahili*, Vol. 48/1, pp. 57-73.

Katupha, J.M.M., 1994, 'The Language Situation and Language Use in Mozambique', in R. Fardon and G. Furniss (eds.) *African Languages, Development and the State*, London and New York: Routledg, pp.89-96.

Kenya Institute of Education (K.I.E), 1986, *Secondary History and Government*, Nairobi: Kenya Literature Bureau.

Ndambuki, J.M., 2001, 'Language use in Democratisation: The Case of Voting Behaviour Among the Akamba Women of Makueni District-Kenya', PhD. Research Proposal, Egerton University, Kenya.

Maake, N.P., 1994, 'Dismantling the Tower of Babel, In Search of a New Language Policy for a Post-Apartheid South Africa', in R. Fardon and G. Furniss (eds.) *African Languages, Development and the State*, London and New York: Routledge pp. 111-121.

Mazrui, A.A. and Mazrui, A.M., 1995, *Swahili State and Society, The Political Economy of an African Language*, Nairobi: East African educational Publishers.

Mukama, R., 1992, 'Behind the Growing Regionalization and Internationalisation of Kiswahili', Makerere Papers, *A Journal of the Department of Languages and Linguistics*, Vol. 1 No. 2.

Ndegwa, P., 1986, *The African Challenge. In Search of Appropriate Development Strategies*, Nairobi: Heinemann Kenya.

Ng'andu, P.M., 1998, 'Globalisation and African Regional Integration', Paper for the 1998 ADB Annual Meetings Symposium on Regional Cooperation and Integration in Africa, Abidjan, Côte d'Ivoire. Available online www.adb.org

Okwany, A., 1995, *Attitudes of High School Students in Kenya Toward the Learning of Kiswahili*, M.A., Chuo Kikuu cha New Brunswick, Canada.

Ohly, R., 1977, 'Swahili: To be a World-Language', *Swahili Studies*, A Supplement to *Kiswahili*, Tol. 47/1. pp. 119-128.

Phillipson, R. and Skutnabb-Kangas, T., 1995, 'Language Rights in Postcolonial Africa', in, S. Tove, P. Robert and Rannut Mart, (eds.), *Linguistic Human Rights: Overcoming Linguistic Discrimination*, Berlin and New York: Mouton de Gruyter, pp. 335-345.

Ravenhill, J., 1985, 'The Future of Regionalism in Africa', in R.I. Onwuka & A. Sesay (eds.) *The Future of Regionalism in Africa*, London and Basingstoke: Macmillan Publishers, pp. 205-224.

4

Language and the East African Parliament: National Identities, Gender Mainstreaming and the Re-invention of Regionalism

Felicia Arudo Yieke

Introduction

East Africa is one African region that enjoys a bounty of African languages. Each of the East African countries has a substantial number of languages, and Kenya for example has about forty different languages with at least two hundred different dialects. Once these countries went through colonialism and obtained their independence (which was roughly around the same time), the linguistic landscape took a new turn. This was in view of the fact that the colonisers, who were in this case British, brought with them their language, English, and imposed it on the young independent nations. Henceforth, these countries had to develop a language policy. Kenya for instance adopted English as an official language, Kiswahili as a national language and about forty languages serving as regional 'tribal' languages (Swahili was later on also given an official language status, although attitudinal changes and readjustments have continued to dog the status of Swahili in this region). In Uganda, English is an official Language, whereas in Tanzania, Swahili is both a national and an official language.

In order to make regional integration a reality, the East African community was formed. This move began at independence. At this point in time, the working language for the community was English. Unfortunately, the community was disbanded in 1977. There has however been a revival of cooperation, and in addition there has been the creation of the East African parliament that is supposed to chart the way forward for the countries in the East African region in terms of social, economic and political improvement of the states. The question now asked is this: against the current linguistic background, which language will be adopted as the working language for the region, and significantly in the East African parliament?

The language question becomes an important issue for several reasons. Firstly, and as already indicated, this region is highly multilingual, boasting of very many East African languages. Some are mutually intelligible, whereas others are not. Secondly, Language can act as a very important agent for conflict resolution. In the search of national and regional renewal, language then is one issue that has to be dealt with if we have to make this renewal a reality, especially in the face of multilingualism. Thirdly, in most cases the common language adopted after independence was English. Do all the concerned parties accept the position of English? What about the ideological loading that is associated with language and English in particular, and especially at a time when Africa is at pains to assert its independence? In adopting the English language, is there anything at stake in terms of national identity? What advantages and disadvantages then would we be dealing with in case of the choice of the English language that is already being used? What other options do we have in the choice of a language? At the same time, whichever language is unanimously accepted as the working language, how are we supposed to deal with the derogatory aspect of language, as far as gender is concerned? This is the fourth reason why the language issue becomes compelling to look at. With these issues in mind, it becomes apparent that the language question can neither be ignored nor be over-emphasised because it is an issue that must be addressed. We thus have to deal with the tensions that come out quite objectively, especially if we need to come up with workable ideas concerning the role of language in the search for national and regional renewal, and yet maintain national identity. It is observed that different countries in this region have various language policies, which lead to different effects, as indeed there are different language policies all over the world.

Language Policy as Guide?

In the choice of a common language, different policies have to be taken into consideration. We can thus identify three different policies leading to diverse effects. The first one is where a local language is performing both official and national functions in such a way that a language such as English has either no function or very little function. This has been the linguistic situation in Tanzania, where Swahili has taken over from English in many spheres. A different policy is where a local language is used as national language and English takes over as the official language. This leaves English with an important function as can be seen in Kenya (and probably in Uganda?). In Kenya however, there are overlapping roles between both Swahili and English. A third language policy is a situation where English is the official language and no specific local language is raised to the status of a national language. In this case, English has a wide range of functions and it enjoys a national status against any local languages. Could Uganda fall within this policy as well?

In the case of Swahili in Kenya, there is certainly no debate. Swahili indeed is accepted as the national language with immense official functions as well. How about Uganda? The problem in this country is partly one of attitude, which it is gratifying to note, is slowly changing. Swahili in this region was despised at one point in history because it was the language used by the military, embodied in the person of the late Idi Amin Dada, whom very few Ugandans wished to recall with any fondness. This in a way stigmatised the language, and as one of the languages of 'the oppressor', nobody wanted to be associated or identified with it. Happily as already said, this attitude is fast changing and this might be for the good of the region and the language as well.

Against the backdrop of different language policies, the truth is that we recognise the importance of English in the region. However, despite this, there have been moves in different parts of the world (this region included) to include local languages in schools in the lower primary and also extend the practice to the higher levels and even tertiary levels as both service subjects and academic subjects. How then would the different policies be affected in as far as Swahili and English are concerned? At the same time, in the face of growing nationalism and political winds of change all over the African region, local languages have been used in literature, and English has been rejected in certain areas. A good example would be Ngugi wa Thiongo's *Decolonising the Mind* (1986), where he encouraged the use of vernacular. The question thus asked is this: Will these moves have an effect on the range of functions of English? How do they impact on Swahili for that matter? I would like to argue that there are crucial reasons why English will continue to be used despite these moves.

The first reason is that English is used all over the world on a functional basis, and for as long as we have both a national and international agenda for our countries, we will continue to use English. In its status as an international language, English is seen as important by both the native and non-native speaker. ('Native' in this sense is not used in its derogatory aspect, but as in the case of a first language speaker or what we call in linguistics the L1). It must be noted that English is no longer tied down to one culture, and today, we can no longer speak of English as the language of the colonialist. Salman Rushdie (quoted in Crystal 1997) says that it is always not necessary to take up the anti-colonial or postcolonial cudgels against English. Instead, he argues that those people who were once colonised are now rapidly remaking English, domesticating it and becoming more and more relaxed about the way they use it. This has been made more possible due to the English language's enormous flexibility and extent. English is thus functional to us as Africans, and we readjust it according to our needs. That is why we have Kenyan English, Ugandan English and Tanzanian English, and yet when we all meet as speakers of 'our Englishes', we are still able to interact and communicate easily. At the same time we can maintain our national identities, and still recognise the fact that the speaker has characteristics in his/her speech that suggest which region he/she comes from, for example Kenyan English, Ugandan English or Tanzanian English. These varieties are respected as non-native varieties of English, and at no any time should they be confused with the native varieties which originate from the UK, the USA, Australia, Canada, parts of Liberia and South Africa. Maybe at this point, we would ask the question whether speaking of English has made us less Kenyan, or less Tanzanian, or less Ugandan or even less East African. If the answer is in the affirmative, then there is need for concern, but if it is in the negative, then English usage does not become problematic!

The second reason why English will continue to be used despite these moves is also connected to the first reason. This is the fact that the language is no longer tied down to one culture (the British culture). Over time, it has gone through a process of 'deculturalisation'. Consequently, English is viewed as a neutral language among a wider diversity of languages and their varieties. The truth is that these regions and the East Africa included, may still need English for a long time to come.

In the face of competing languages in the region such as Swahili and English, an important factor for the preservation of either language in the face of varying controversies onto which language to choose, is one of attitude. Kachru (1982) refers to this as 'Attitudinal Re-adjustment', and says that this is the responsibility of the non-native speaker of the English language. He thus gives us a guideline on how to go about 'attitudinal readjustment', which we look at in the next section.

The Importance of Attitudinal (Re) Adjustments in the Choice of Language

Firstly, the non-native speakers of English of which we from the East African region are a part of, must disassociate English from our colonial past, and no longer treat it as a tool of colonialism and colonial oppression, but as functional in our various contexts.

Secondly, the non-native speaker of English should avoid seeing English as an influence in westernising users (English is not synonymous with westernisation), thus forfeiting African cultural practices (we must however submit that culture is usually a part and parcel of language). However, in the case of English as it is and has grown today, no one single culture can lay claim to it, especially when we see the language in terms of the concentric circles which Kachru (1982) and Crystal (1997) refer to in terms of the Inner circle, the Outer circle and the Expanding circle. People who acquire English as a native language fall within the inner circle, whereas people who acquire English as a second language fall within the outer circle, and people who acquire English as a foreign language fall within the expanding circle. Both the outer circle and the expanding circle, which are the non-native varieties, have adopted English for their linguistic situations and cultures. Salman Rushdie (quoted in Crystal 1997:130) in his essay 'Commonwealth Literature does not exist' remarks that the English Language actually ceased to be the sole possession of the English sometime ago. No one can now claim sole ownership.

Thirdly, the non-native variety of English users should accept that there is a large literature in English written by African speakers as part of the non-native tradition. In any case, if you read the African writers' series books, the writers are able to articulate their ideas and cultures very well in their own varieties of English. They have managed to 'Africanise' their English and even make their own coinages to suit their situations. For example, there is the case of the word 'Unbwogable', which was used during the last multiparty elections in Kenya in 2002, and became quite popular across a broad spectrum of Kenyans. (The root of the word 'bwogo' is Dholuo [a Kenyan language] and refers to one who is invincible and cannot be shaken or cowed despite all. The prefix un- and suffix -able are both from English). Chinua Achebe (quoted in Crystal 1997) provides a strong argument on the use of English by African writers. He says that the price a world language must be prepared to pay is submission to many different kinds of use. The African writer should aim to use English in a way that brings out his/her message best without altering the language to the extent that its value as a medium of international exchange is lost. He adds that the writer should aim at fashioning an English, which is at once universal and able to carry out his/her peculiar experience. Achebe thus feels that English will be able to carry the weight of his own African experience, but it will have to be a new English, still in full communion with its ancestral home but altered to suit its new African surroundings.

Fourthly, the non-native users of English should be out to develop a variety of the non-native varieties of English without the feeling that these are inferior. These models should function much as the indigenous languages do.

Fifthly, it is important to distinguish the functions of the language in terms of both the national and internal uses ('nationism') of English in the region. It is important also to note that it is the nationalist functions, which ultimately contribute to the non-native varieties. It is this fifth guideline on which we will now concentrate when we consider critically the linguistic positioning of language (whether English, Swahili or any other language) in this East African region, and specifically for our East African Parliament. We thus examine two concepts critically. The first is Nationality (Nationalism) and the second is Nation, which gives rise to Nationism. However, we will first look at the concepts of Nation, National identities and the centrality of language.

The Concept of Nation, National Identities and the Centrality of Language

In the investigation of national identities, we need to consider a few basic assumptions, which De Cilia et al (1999) also examine, before we look at the idea of a nation. Firstly, we start from the assumption that nations are to be understood as mental constructs and are larger than face-to-face groups. They are what Anderson (1991, 1988:15) calls 'imagined political communities'. These mental constructs are represented in the minds and memories of the nationalised subjects as sovereign and limited political units, and can become very influential guiding ideas with sometimes serious and destructive consequences. Members of even the smallest nations do not know the majority of their fellow citizens, do not meet and do not hear from one another, and yet they are convinced that they belong to a unique national community. Nations are perceived as limited by boundaries and thereby cut off from the surrounding nations, because no nation identifies with humanity in its entirety. The nation is thus perceived as a community of congenial similars and regarded as sovereign, which partly can be traced back to its secular 'roots' in the era of the 'Enlightenment'.

Secondly, we assume that national identities, which are conceived as specific forms of social identities are, by means of language and other semiotic system, discursively produced, reproduced, transformed and restructured. The idea of a specific national community becomes a reality in the realm of convictions and beliefs through reifying, figurative discourses continually launched by politicians, intellectuals and media people and disseminated through the systems of education, schooling, mass communication, militarisation and so on.

The third assumption draws on Pierre Bourdieu's (1992, 1991) notion of habitus. National identity can be regarded as a sort of habitus, that is to say, as a complex of common ideas, concepts or perception scheme of (a) related emotional attitudes intersubjectively shared within a specific group of people, as well as of (b) similar behavioural dispositions, all of which (c) are internalised through national socialisation. The emotional attitudes to which Bourdieu refers are those manifested towards the specific national 'in-group' on the one hand, and respective 'out-group' on the other. Behavioural dispositions include both dispositions towards solidarity with one's own national group as well as the readiness to exclude the 'others' from this constructed collective, and to debase them.

Fourthly, the discursive construction of nations and national identities always runs hand in hand with the construction of difference/distinctiveness as uniqueness (Hall 1994, 1996; Martin 1995). As soon as it is elevated to an imaginary collective level, both the construction of sameness and the construction of difference violate pluralistic and democratic variety and multiplicity by group internal homogenisation (of in-groups as well as out-groups).

The fifth assumption is that there is no such thing as the one and only national identity in an essentialised sense, but rather that different identities are discursively constructed according to context; that is according to the social field, the situational setting of the discursive act and the topic to be discussed. In other words, national identities are not completely consistent, stable and immutable. They are, to the contrary, to be understood as dynamic, fragile, 'vulnerable' and often incoherent. However, we do assume that there are certain relations between the image of identity offered by political elites or the media, and everyday discourses about nations and national identities. In addition to these assumptions, the construction of national identity builds on the emphasis on a common history, and history has always to do with remembrance and memory. The notion of 'collective memory' thus becomes important here. This implies the selective recollection of past events that are thought to be important for the members of a specific community, which allows one to reify abstract, ideational concepts. Apart from the role of history, Hall (1994) emphasises the role culture plays in the construction of nations and national identities. Hall describes nations not only as political constructs, but also as 'systems of cultural representations', by means of which an imagined community may be interpreted. People are not only citizens by law; they also participate in forming the idea of the nation as it is represented in their national culture. A nation is thus a symbolic community constructed discursively. What all these mean is that the issue of language is of utmost importance to the construction of a national identity, and should not be ignored when we look at the language question within the East African region. We now turn to nationality and nation as determining factors in the choice of language.

Nationality and 'Nationism' as Determining Factors in the Choice of Language

A nationality is a group of people who think of themselves as a social unit, different from one group but not on a purely local scale. Nationality might thus be distinguished from an ethnic group, which is like a nationality, but it is smaller, simpler, more particular, and is more localised. As far as Nationalism is concerned therefore, language serves the purpose of contrastive self-identity: referring to members of a nationality who have united with others to speak one language, and are distinct from people who do not speak that language.

One important aspect of nationality is that it does not have an independent territory of its own. It is in a way neutral since its existence is devoid of an independent political boundary. Modern boundaries may therefore sociologically mean very little to people who think of themselves as nationalistic. What this implies is that as much as the individual East African countries can each be seen as separate nations, we can also look at this East African region in a nationalist way, thus making it easier to prescribe an agenda for it. In respect to nationalism, language together with culture, religion and history is a major component. Language thus serves as a link with the glorious past and authenticity. Language here is part of the history itself and it would be advantageous to the nationality to have a language of its own (i.e. at a lower level as one East African country, for example Swahili in Kenya, or at a larger level within the East Africa). The question arises: which language in East Africa should serve this function? Could Swahili work?

Nationism on the other hand is concerned with more political problems of governing. In fact the function of language in terms of nationism is in the area of national administration, government and communication between the government and its people. In this sense of nationism, the language may also be used as a medium of instruction that effectively transmits knowledge to children in schools.

The two distinctions (nationalism and nationism) that we have tried to explain so far bear on the functions of language in society. By looking at these functions, we can begin to critically think and make informed choices on which languages would be suited for what situations and would help to put the language debate in Africa to a comfortable rest, especially so regarding the imminent rivalry between Swahili and English language usage. For this reason, we should briefly go through both the official functions and the nationalist functions and decide which language would be best for what particular situation: look at it from a wider framework, and also from the framework of the East African parliament.

Once declared an official language (nationism), that language must also:

- Serve as language for written communication between government agents, at the national level i.e. between the ministries.

- Serve as spoken language of the government officials in their duties at national level.

- Be the language in which government records are kept.

- Be the language in which laws and regulations governing the nation are originally written and may later be translated (to reach the grassroots).

- Be the language in which official forms related to government business are published at the initial stage.

It is however important to note that an official language may perform some and not all the above tasks and this may depend on the degree of 'officiality'. At the same time, it is also possible to have more than one language performing the same task. In order to perform official functions, the language should have undergone a degree of standardisation. It should also have a group to speak it, and this group should be well distributed geographically, although it could also be a small group of the population.

Although a language may serve both official and national functions, these functions should be clearly stated and kept apart. The national language should be able to serve the following nationalist functions:

- It should serve as a symbol of national identity for a large part of the population.
- It can be used for some everyday official function by many of the population although not as regularly.
- Many people must speak the language fluently and with ease.
- The language must be accepted as a symbol of authenticity. It must be "good enough" and its credibility as an authentic language must imply a high degree of standardisation.
- Finally, a language in its nationalist function must be seen as a link with the glorious past of the country or region.

The debate over the choice of one African language as against English, or vice versa, has been a contentious one for a long time. However, once we delineate these roles and functions, we may be in the process of sorting out these controversies, and choice no longer becomes a difficulty. If we want to choose a language for the Parliament, we must first and foremost ask ourselves the functions of Parliament. If these functions are in line with nationalist ideals, then we would probably choose a language such as Swahili. However, if the functions bring out the nationism dimension, then we would look no further and develop our 'East African English', which inevitably must be standardised in spite of it being a localised variety. Despite the language having initially been 'imported' from the outside, it has grown immensely to an extent where we can say that it has been localised and nativised to articulate our needs and desires as a people, without actually losing our sense of self and national identity, and still be able to articulate issues of national and regional integration.

It is thus my submission that English will still be used for a long time to come. However, the importance of languages like Swahili cannot be ignored and should be developed alongside English to enable them to be functional as much as possible in the region. On this account, the change in attitude (attitudinal readjustment) is of utmost importance if we have to make these realities.

On Gender Mainstreaming in the East African Parliament

At this point, we should also make a comment on Gender Mainstreaming within the Parliament. How are we supposed to deal with the derogatory aspect of language in as far as gender is concerned? We must remember that parliament is made up of both men and women members who are supposed to be articulating the needs of both genders in the region. We should thus sit and rewrite the language to make it more gender friendly and gender neutral as much as possible.

Gender mainstreaming may involve many social and political factors (Wodak 2002). However, for this particular paper, we are concerned with the linguistic aspect. There has been a desire to change the patriarchal and sexist nature of language, and therefore engage in various types of linguistic reform or language planning. Creating a women-centred language capable of expressing reality from women's perspective is one objective, which calls for feminist language planning (Cameron 1998; Doyle 1998; Pauwels 1998a & 1998b; Kramarae & Treichler 1990). At the same time, there is the 'linguistic equality of the sexes' approach, which has become synonymous with feminist language planning in the eyes of the wider community. Linguistic discrimination is seen as a form of sex discrimination, which can be addressed in ways similar to other forms of sex discrimination (e.g. in employment). The prominence of the linguistic equality approach is also due to the media attention to non-sexist language guidelines, which is the main instrument of promoting this type of gender-sensitive language reform (Perry et al 1992; Doyle 1998; Ehrlich & King 1992).

Advocates of the linguistic equality approach use the strategies of gender-neutralisation (sometimes referred to as gender abstraction) and/or gender-specification (feminisation) to attain their goal of creating a language, which allows for a balanced representation of the sexes. Gender neutralisation on the one hand, involves minimising or eliminating gender specific expressions and constructions. It entails that any morpho-syntactic and lexical features marking human agent nouns and pronouns (or other parts of speech) as masculine or feminine are 'neutralised' for gender, especially in generic contexts (Pauwels 1998a:109). Examples for English include among others:

- The elimination of gender-suffix of -ess, -ette, in relation to human agent nouns as in Hostess, Usherette, Authoress. These suffixes tend to trivialise the person and occupation.

- The creation of compound nouns involving 'person' as in chairperson, tradesperson, spokesperson as opposed to chairman, tradesman and spokesman respectively.

- The avoidance of the generic 'he'.

Gender specification on the other hand, also known as feminisation, is a strategy used to achieve linguistic equality by making the 'invisible sex' (in most cases women) visible in language through systematic and symmetrical marking of gender. Although English does not use this strategy much (it is found more often in languages with grammatical gender), the use of 'he' or 'she' and of such phrases as policewomen and policemen, actors and actresses in generic contexts exemplifies the gender specification strategy.

Underlying the linguistic equality approach to reform is a belief that making changes to linguistic reforms will contribute significantly to the promotion of non-sexist meanings. This will go a long way towards the gender mainstreaming exercise within the East African parliament even as deliberations are made as to how best to run the affairs of the East African region.

Conclusion

As we conclude, we realise that language issues are actually quite contentious and problematic and can also become very emotional since we are dealing with issues of self and national identities, which impinge greatly on the language question. This means that the language question is one that has to be treated carefully as we deliberate on which language to choose for the East African region, and specifically for the East African Parliament. This consideration has to be taken into account if we are to realise our objectives insofar as the re-invention of regionalism and integration is concerned. The issues therefore raised in the paper are of central importance; i.e. language policy, the concept of nation, national identities and their centrality to language, the notion of nationalism vis-à-vis nationism, the need for attitudinal readjustments in language issues, and the importance of gender mainstreaming in parliament in as far as the linguistic aspect is concerned. These issues will inform future deliberations on the choice of language, and probably on coming to a consensus on 'Which Language?'

References

Anderson, Benedict, 1991, *Imagined Communities: Reflections on the Origin and Spread of Nationalism*, London: Verso.

Anderson, Benedict, 1988, *Die Erfindung der Nation: Zur Karrier eines folgenreichen Konzepts*, Frankfurt: Campus.

Bourdieu, Pierre, 1992 [1991], *Language and Symbolic Power*, London: Polity Press.

Cameron, Deborah, 1998, 'Lost in Translation. Non Sexist Language', in D. Cameron, (ed.), *The Feminist Critique of Language*, London: Routledge.

De Cilia, Rudolf, Reisigl, Martin & Wodak, Ruth, 1999, 'The Discursive Construction of National Identity', *Discourse and Society*, 10 (2) 149–173.

Crystal, David, 1997, *English as a Global Language*, Cambridge: CUP.

Doyle, Margaret, 1998, 'Introduction to the A-Z of Non-Sexist Language', in Deborah Cameron, ed., *The Feminist Critique of Language*, London: Routledge.

Ehrlich, Susan & King, Ruth, 1992, 'Gender Based Language Reform and the Social Construction of Meaning', *Discourse and Society*, 3/2. 151-166.

Hall, Stuart. 1996, 'Introduction: Who needs "Identity?"', in Stuart Hall & P. Du Gay (eds.), *Questions of Cultural Identity*, Social Identities 1 (1): 5-20.

Hall, Stuart, 1994, *Rassismus und Kulturelle Identität*. Ausgewählte Schriften 2. Hamburg: Argument (Argument Sonderband 226).

Kachru, Braj, ed., 1982, *The Other Tongue: English Across Cultures*, Oxford: Pergamon Press.

Kramarae Cheris & Paula Treichler, 1990, 'Words on a Feminist Dictionary', in Deborah Cameron (ed.) (1st edition) *The Feminist Critique of Language*, London: Routledge.

Martin, D.C., 1995, 'The Choices of Identity', *Social Identities* 1 (1): 5-20.

Mohochi, Ernest, 2002, 'Language and Regional Integration: Foreign or African Language for the African Union', Paper Presented at the 10th General Assembly in Kampala Uganda 8–12 December 2002.

Pauwels, Anne, 1998a, *Women Changing Language*, London: Routledge.

Pauwels, Anne, 1998b, 'Feminist Language Planning: Has it been worthwhile?' *Linguistic Online*, 1, 1/98. http://viadrina.euv-frankfurt-o-de/~wjournal/heft1-99/pauwels.htm

Perry, Linda, Lynn Turner & Helen Sterk, eds.,1992, 'Avoiding Sexism in Communication Research: Guidelines for Gender/Sex Research and Publication', in Linda Perry et.al, *Constructing and Reconstructing Gender: The Links Among Communication, Language and Gender*, New York: SUNY, pp.295-301.

Platt, J., 1984, *The New Englishes*, London: Routledge and Kegan Paul.

Wa' Thiongo, Ngugi, 1986, *Decolonising the Mind: The Politics of Language in African Literature*, Nairobi: East African Educational Publishers Ltd.

Wodak, Ruth, 2002, 'Interdisciplinarity, Gender Studies and CDA: Gender Mainstreaming and the European Union', Plenary lecture presented at International Gender and Language Association (IGALA2) at Lancaster University. 12–14 April 2002.

5

Ethnicity: An Opportunity or a Bane in Africa's Development?

Emmanuel Okoth Manyasa

Introduction: Ethnicity in Africa

This paper examines the issue of ethnicity in Africa and highlights the various threats to, and opportunities for Africa's development that arise from it. For a long time, ethnic diversity in Africa has been blamed for various undesirable outcomes. The successive periods of turmoil in Uganda between 1962 and 1986 were largely attributed to it. The 'culture of eating' by the ruling ethnic groups brewed discontent among the marginalized groups and gave birth to resistance, leading to wars and the overthrow of regimes (Okalany 1996). In Kenya, politicians exploited long-standing ethnic tensions to foment the infamous violence labelled 'tribal clashes' of the 1990s (Kenya Human Rights Commission 1998).

While these episodes of violence remain as sores on our civic body, always stirring up vengeful thoughts in the minds of the victims, this paper notes with concern that African leaders have by design chosen to downplay the reality that is ethnicity in Africa. Whenever they have an opportunity to comment on this issue, the temptation to moralise and posture for the audience overwhelms them. Most leaders put on masks to conceal the naked tribalism that often escapes their guard through affirmative and dismissive grins and frowns as they struggle to maintain their presumed moral high ground. Some leaders have in their ignorance even attempted to suppress individual ethnic languages in the hope of suppressing ethnicity. Yet this process has the potential to undermine the nation-state (Simala 1996). As a consequence of this posturing, the discussion and legislation on this issue has tended to be more abstract than pragmatic. Because of pretences surrounding the issue of ethnicity, there is unmitigated ethnocentrism that is inimical to the sustainability of most African states, as we know them today.

As the social, political and religious leaders do everything to sweep ethnicity under the carpet in a futile attempt to wish it away, it is my considered submission that a time has come when Africa must confront ethnicity. There is an identity crisis in Africa today (Youth Agenda 2002). Ethnic and national loyalties are in competition and conflict. Ethnic ambitions have quickly replaced national loyalties in most African states. On any national issue, despite pretences at moral and intellectual arguments, anybody can see the tribal orientation of the debaters. The ongoing constitutional review process in Kenya is one such example where one can predict a person's argument by his or her surname.

In African multiparty elections, ethnic labels have acquired more salience than either policy or ideology. An African voter is a member of an ethnic group first and a worker or a bourgeois second. One example can illustrate this tendency. In 1992, Oginga Odinga, a longtime opponent of the KANU regime in Kenya, tried to marshal support from the disadvantaged Kenyan voters. But when he turned to see who were following him, it was not disadvantaged Kenyans from all ethnic groups, it was Luos of all social classes (Mazrui 1994). The same was the case for Kenneth Matiba, who was likewise followed by fellow Kikuyus from all strata of society. Even the clergy owe more allegiance to their ethnic groups than to the churches in which they minister. Examples of this abound from the role of the clergy in the Rwandan genocide, to the sudden change in behaviour of certain prominent clergymen in Kenya since the 2002 general elections.

Liberal democracy, which is one of the most important Western ideological legacies in Africa, has not improved ethnic relations in most countries. It has, in the short run, served to heighten competitive ethnic consciousness, ethnicise political competition, increase ethnic tensions, generate conflicts, and promote separatism (Mazrui 1994). This has eroded any gains against ethnocentrism from liberal capitalism, which is yet another important legacy of the West in Africa. While capitalism promotes individualism and a class struggle that begins to erode tribal allegiance, it is exploitative, creating selective areas of poverty. It is also open to abuse and, indeed, it has been abused to reinforce ethnic dominance that quite naturally, brews discontent and stirs rebellion.

Ethno-politics is not just an African problem though. Ethnic problems would obtain if the Second World War had artificially reorganised European borders by partitioning the existing nations into new territories, each comprising part of the previously existing countries. For example, in a country carved out of part of Spain, part of France and part of Italy, the struggle for power would take place between the Spanish party, the French party and the Italian party, rather than on an ideological or a programme basis. The same 'tribal' considerations would in all likelihood dominate politics in such a hypothetical country artificially created out of parts of existing European states. The violence and 'ethnic cleansing' in former Yugoslavia in 1995 demonstrates that Europeans are not immune to 'tribalism' even now.

Africa, the worst hit continent by this problem, must wake up to the reality that ethnicity will face this continent until the end of time. And that as Kimenyi (1989) correctly puts it, the degree of ethnic heterogeneity in any given country will remain fairly constant for a long time to come, courtesy of the irrational partition of Africa by the colonialists. They must then resolve to confront it with more practicable strategies than the current hypocritical approaches being employed by those in positions of influence.

Perhaps at this point, it is important to pause and ask two pertinent questions. First, what is ethnicity and second, how did it permeate our society so deeply? According to Tumin (1964), an ethnic group is a group of people defined by a complex of traits drawn from religious and linguistic characteristics, who have distinctive skin pigmentation, besides a common national or geographic origin. According to Okundiba (1978), it is the communal character of the people that puts them together as an ethnic group, making language the most important identity for any such group. Hasu (1973) on the other hand defines an ethnic group as the psychosocial race, which is critical in understanding values, behaviours and policies. Hameso (1997) defines an ethnic group as a community of people characterised by three main features, which distinguish them from others. These features are (i) the occupation of a physical space and emotional attachment to this space no matter where they find themselves; (ii) a common language and myth of common descent; and (iii) common culture.

Tribalism in its present form in Africa is not a traditional aspect of African culture. It is but a product of the development imposed on the continent by colonialism. Colonialism and the social and economic changes it brought with it 'created' the sense of tribalism and strong ethnic identities that are present in modern Africa. Tribes were created as a means to gain power, resources and recognition in the process of colonial modernising. The term 'tribe,' (which is the pejorative reference to ethnic group), was first used in Africa two centuries ago, when Europeans began to move into the interior of Africa for the first time. They used this term to describe the groups of Africans with whom they came into contact because they thought that all non-European peoples organised themselves into 'tribes'. Such groups they considered less modern, even 'primitive,' in comparison to 'nation-states,' that was the form of organisation in the 19th Century Europe (Hameso 1997).

The assumption that the tribes had clear boundaries and consisted of culturally identical peoples became the basis for tribal creation, as the missionaries especially, and other state institutions sought to formalise and categorise these tribal units. The erroneous belief that African societies were 'tribal' in structure influenced the way in which colonial governance was organised. Colonial politics in turn helped to create the ethnic social organisations that have become dominant in most African countries. Beginning with the conquest of Africa, European powers depended on strategies of 'divide and conquer' and then employed 'divide and rule' to sustain themselves in power. In gaining control of African colonies, European powers often played one nation or kingdom against another.

Once colonial rule was established, colonial governments accentuated differences between ethnic groups making them suspicious of each other. For a system that plays one group against another to work, it has to benefit one group more than it benefits others. The privileged and disadvantaged groups then naturally become acrimonious rivals, with the former pursuing preservation as the later pursues reform. This tactic of divide and rule therefore helped to establish a political system that promoted divisions based on ethnicity, rather than unity based on a common national identity.

This externally imposed division of the African people was temporarily overcome by the surge in nationalist movements after the World War II. The quintessence of nationalism was, and is, anti-imperialism. It was a struggle against, rather than for something. It was an expression of a struggle against denial; denial of humanity, denial of respect and dignity, denial of the Africanness of the African (Cabral 1980). Africans sought the right to make their own decisions, the right to self-determination. The desire for this freedom superseded the deep-seated differences cultivated amongst them by their colonial masters. This urge by Africans to free themselves bolstered the nationalist and Pan-Africanist movements, leading to the liberation of most African states by early 1980s.

At independence, which connoted the liberation of the state however, nationalism and Pan-Africanism were edged out of most African countries by the resurrection of a negative ethnicity. This scenario was precipitated by the failure of the respective independent African governments to be, as Cabral puts it, 'liberation movements in power'. They abandoned the core objective of the nationalist project, which according to Shivji (2002), was and still is, the right of the people to self-determination. An emergent national bourgeoisie abused state power and betrayed national sovereignty by preferring to identify with the Western bourgeoisie, from whom they learnt their lessons.

Having captured state power, and keen on self-perpetuation, they employ the same colonial tactics of divide and rule. As a consequence, a trend towards ethnocracy has set in and ethnic-governing classes have emerged in most countries. The best jobs, the best land and the best commercial opportunities are disproportionately distributed to the privileged ethnic governing class. In return, the favoured ethnic groups shield the leaders from public scrutiny. The rivalries initiated in the colonial era have been invigorated and ethnic prejudices perpetuated by the governing ethnic groups. Indeed, ethnicity has become one of the defining characteristics of post-colonial politics in Africa. In multi-ethnic nations, ethnic apartheid usually involves discrimination in favour of the governing ethnic group, while in dual ethnic nations, it involves discrimination against the other ethnic group.

Ethnocratic regimes ignore the realities of the artificiality of the nation-state in Africa, and insist on highly centralised forms of government purely out of selfish interests, since autocracy works better in highly centralised systems. With a highly centralised state, the leader of the ethnic group that captures the state has control over an enormous amount of resources, which the leader appropriates disproportionately to his or her ethnic group. Instead of unifying the various ethnic groups, centralised unitary states have provided leaders with opportunities to extend benefits to some groups at the expense of other groups.

The worst legacy of colonialism in Africa, however, was handed down in form of the arbitrary if not malicious partition of Africa into units that do not meet the criteria of existence as nation-states. The colonialists, whose interests were to parcel out, own and exploit Africa, disregarded the ethnic and demographic realities of Africa's inhabitants. An anonymous Canadian researcher, who is very pessimistic about the future of social and economic development in Africa wrote: 'The tragedy of Africa is that three centuries of overwhelming colonial interference have left most countries a medley of tribes, foreign one to another with only a few cases of ethnic territorial concentration, where coherent communities could possibly meet the conditions for creating nation-states (identifiable territory, critical mass and distinct ethnic and cultural identity)' (www.ethnicity.net/research).

The partition of Africa resulted in many situations whereby members of the same ethnic group were separated and placed in different countries. Members of the Somali community for example found themselves dispersed into Somalia, Ethiopia and Kenya. The Iteso and the Luhyia found themselves in Kenya and Uganda; the Maasai in Kenya and Tanzania; the Yoruba and the Aja were dispersed into Nigeria, Benin and Togo; the Wolof and the Serers between Senegal and the Gambia. The political units that were created were not only arbitrary, but also lacked any strong unifying factors. Given the features of ethnicity, which include a common consciousness of being one in relation to other relevant groups and exclusiveness, where acceptance and rejection on linguistic and cultural grounds characterise social relations, this arbitrary partition was enough recipe for lasting problems.

Threats of Ethnicity to African Development

Much of the development discourse on Africa has painted a picture of gloom, lending credence to the global perception of Africa as a hopeless continent from which nothing good can come. Most African countries only appear on the global stage to present their unrivalled HIV/AIDS prevalence rates. Many more are only heard of when they are bleeding from ethnically motivated internal conflicts and therefore seeking western (international) intervention. Indeed many commentators consider Africa, a continent that is trapped in a vicious cycle of 'ethnicity-bad governance-poor economic performance-ethnicity'.

Looking at the voting patterns in multiparty elections in Africa today, one gets the impression that the foremost factor in African politics is and will probably remain the ethnic origin of the politicians rather than their ideology or their policies for improving the society's well being. The tribal leader who ascends to national leadership through such an election is expected to channel part of the largesse from the civic public to the primordial public. In the land where people identify more closely with their tribe than with the country, it is natural that the object of achieving political power is to further the interests of one's own ethnic group rather than to ensure the maximum social and economic development for all the people.

This context leads quite naturally to ethnic favouritism, intolerance of political opposition (which is largely ethnic rather than ideological), to arbitrary rule, to the disregard for human rights and finally, to the widespread nepotism and corruption which are the major operational obstacles to economic and social development in most African states. It also encourages mediocrity in leadership where people vote for 'one of their own' whether or not he or she has the moral and intellectual credentials to ascend to the particular office. Trade unions, political parties and even civil societies, which are supposed to be vehicles for civic mobilisation, become tribal domains, whose leadership is too preoccupied with ethnic scheming and counter-scheming to see to the interests of their suffering masses.

Based upon the collective tribal tradition, most institutions that set the moral code of conduct leave no room for personal responsibility. This explains to a large extent why the irresponsible men and women who ascend to leadership positions in this continent are often shielded by their ethnic groups from public scrutiny. Members of the so called 'ruling ethnic groups' even put their lives on the line in defence of these despots, which quite naturally, offends other ethnic groups, often exploding into ethnic conflicts that have rocked many African countries.

Ethnic voting patterns reinforce the ethnocracy that rewards those ethnic groups in the ruling coalition and punishes those excluded. In addition, to retain control of the instruments of wealth transfers, those in power have an interest in erecting barriers to entry into political and economic markets. Communities are subjected to economic sabotage by their own governments for the simple reason that they appear to be competing for state power. Or one of 'their own', obviously with their support, is seeking to challenge the incumbent. Governments frustrate foreign direct investments if the investors intend to partner with members of the communities regarded as competing for power with the ruling ethnic group. Ethnocratic considerations override macro-economic prudence, as governments engage in practices that impede proper policy formulation and implementation. The hostile macro-economic environment and the resultant poor performance of the economy trickles down into every household (except those of the ruling elite), in the form of unemployment, poor healthcare, insecurity and ever worsening poverty levels.

There is ample evidence that many African governments have maintained their control of governance structures by redistributing resources in favour of groups such as the military and specific ethnic groups (Hameso 1997). The discriminatory allocation of resources in ethnically divided societies is a primary cause of ethnic conflicts. These conflicts entail enormous costs—a conflict situation lowers economic growth besides diverting huge resources from development uses. In Central and West Africa for example, such resources are estimated at $1 billion and more than $800 million a year respectively (World Bank 2000). These estimates exclude the indirect costs of conflict such as the damage to the welfare of neighbouring countries generated by refugee flows, costs arising from impeded communication routes and the disruption in economic activity.

Conflicts that have plagued the continent have generally been between different ethnic groups within a country. There is clear evidence that conflicts have an ethnic dimension—virtually every African conflict has some ethno-regional dimension to it. Even conflicts that are apparently free of ethnic considerations involve factions and alliances built around ethnic lines (Deng 1997). In Nigeria, there was a conflict between the Ibo people and other ethnic groups in the eastern region of the country, due to the Ibo's unsuccessful secession attempt aimed at forming their own Biafra State. Conflicts in Rwanda and Burundi have been reported as some of the most intense inter-ethnic conflicts in the Third World. They involve the Tutsi and Hutu ethnic groups. Both in Rwanda and Burundi, the Hutu constitute a numerical majority while the minorities Tutsi dominate the countries' economic and political scene. Rivalry between the two is reportedly so intense that each ethnic group has attempted genocide aimed at the complete eradication of the other. In 1972 for example, the Tutsi-controlled government in Burundi killed between 100,000 and 200,000 Hutus in one such incidence of genocide (Hameso 1997).

In Ethiopia, ethnic conflict between the Amhara and Eritreans persisted for hundreds of years as the Eritrean people sought independence from Ethiopia. After independence, their conflict has taken on a new look—from war for autonomy to border war. Similarly, members of the Somali ethnic group have sought independence from the Amhara who have for years dominated the politics and economy of Ethiopia. Other examples of inter-ethnic conflict deteriorating into wars that have claimed the lives of hundreds of thousands of people include Sudan, Mozambique, Somalia, Angola and the Democratic Republic of the Congo.

Conflicts aside, some recent studies also show that corruption tends to be associated with ethnic heterogeneity (Kimenyi and Mbaku 1999). Kimenyi (1989) provides empirical evidence showing that the degree to which African nations are able to establish democratic institutions is greatly influenced by population heterogeneity. In particular, the study shows that the degree of democratisation decreases as ethnic heterogeneity increases. Liberal democracy is bad news for Africa in the short run because multiparty rivalry heightens competitive ethnic consciousness, ethnicises political competition, degenerates into physical political conflict, and sometimes promotes separatism (Mazrui 1994). Ethnicisation has killed thought and reason, dynamism and efficiency, and therefore patriotism. It has destroyed state cohesion and promoted tribalism (Ngenge 1999).

In my opinion, ethnic heterogeneity is a challenge even in the fight against HIV/AIDS in Africa. In as far as the various ethnic groups continue to regard culture as those things that their ancestors used to do, and refuse to recognise that culture is a way of life which must take into account the prevailing circumstances, ethnicity will continue to undermine the war on AIDS. Given the fact that AIDS is a sexually transmitted disease—a taboo subject in most African cultures—the states are unable to formulate and implement policies that could adequately deal with the disease without wrecking the fragile harmonious coexistence of the communities within the various multi-ethnic nations.

All the aforementioned factors undermine sustainable economic development and inhibit the realisation of social justice, which according to Aseka (2003) is the highest in the hierarchy of human needs and the ultimate prize for society's civility. Both liberal democracy and liberal capitalism as envisaged by the western world collapse in the face of ethnicity. Given that ethnic heterogeneity in any one country is predetermined and does not change much over time, the available evidence on social relations among different ethnic groups points to a gloomy future for the ethnically diverse nations of Africa (Kimenyi and Mbaku 1999).

Tapping Ethnic Diversity into Africa's development

Does this mean Africa is down and out? Does the ethnic reality condemn this continent to eternal poverty and underdevelopment? Am I in any way suggesting that the only way to achieve sustainable peace and harmony in this continent is to redraw our national boundaries along ethnic lines? Not at all! In fact I am one of the people who hold the view that Africa has been partitioned into rather too many nation states, making them economically unviable. I am in favour of Africa's integration and not differentiation. In the light of the ethnic question, I share Kimenyi's view that Africa's ethnic problems are due to the failure of political institutions to accommodate diverse interests (ethnic, religious, and linguistic) (Kimenyi 2002). It is this failure that has generated conflict situations that adversely affect political and economic outcomes.

The basic premise of this paper, therefore, is that the ethnic group can be an important institution of collective choice since for many Africans, ethnicity is a source of collective and self identity (Hameso 1997). What is required is a shift in the development paradigm in Africa. The paradigm needs to be refocused on two intertwined sectors of change; the promotion of cultural identity, and the empowerment of the people (Serageldin 1994). Since Africans have demonstrated that they respond more to socio-cultural ideologies (ethnicity, religion, nationalism) than socio-economic ideologies (socialism, labour movements, class solidarity), the development paradigm should take into account the supremacy of culture. Culture, which is rooted in ethnicity, appeals most and makes Africans capable of religious ecumenism as long as it does not reinforce pre-existing ethnic differences (Mazrui 1994).

Every region has cultural manifestations that strike deep responsive chords in the people. They achieve this mainly because they draw upon an authentic heritage that helps define the shared image of the self and society that in turn creates a collectivity. The clarity of that cultural identity and its evolving continuity are essential to create an integrated and integrating cultural framework (Serageldin 1994). Such a cultural framework is a pre-requisite for relevant and effective institutions rooted in authenticity and tradition, yet open to modernity and change, which in turn are imperative for real development to take place. The liberal capitalist legacy of the West that has insisted on individualism, has hampered the existence of such a cultural framework, translating into a lack of national self-confidence and social fragmentation, with a westernised elite and alienated, poor majorities (Serageldin 1994).

Recognising that ethnic units play an important role in the organisation of African societies is crucial in the design of appropriate institutions. Such institutions are imperative in promoting positive ethnicity. Positive ethnicity allays fears and suspicions of other ethnic groups, enhances respect for other cultures, restrains the monopolistic post-colonial state, and facilitates the equitable distribution of resources, all of which can enhance socio-economic progress, justice and democracy. Positive ethnicity can be achieved by respecting and promoting all languages, recognising and formalising ethnicity, accepting the legitimacy of ethnic claims, and by decentralising state institutions (Hameso 1997). These goals can be pursued through the establishment of local ethnic jurisdictions, each possessing a fair degree of autonomy (Kimenyi 2002).

In recent times, ethnic associations provide many services that African states are cutting down on, following donor conditions that require them to minimise expenditure on social services. As a result of the contraction of state supported social services, ethnicity is being reinforced through self-help services such as schools, financial support to bereaved families and campaigns against HIV/AIDS (Hameso 1997). Indeed governments now appreciate that they cannot win the war against AIDS without addressing the rural populations in the languages they understand and regard so dearly. In most East African countries now, one finds in local shopping centres billboards with anti-AIDS messages written in the local languages.

As can be expected, ethnic groups within the same country are likely to be vastly different in terms of their ability to generate a surplus. Each ethnic group can increase its 'ethnic' surplus by entering into mutually beneficial exchange with other ethnic groups. Thus, under conditions whereby ethnic groups are able to freely organise production and enter into market exchange with other groups, each ethnic group would seek to be efficient in production in order to increase its surplus. Note that this is true if the ethnic groups are able to retain their tribal surplus (Kimenyi 1989). Given the distinct features of ethnic groups as compared to other interest groups such as labour unions or producer groups, in that membership in an ethnic group is permanent, ethnic groups are easier interest groups to mobilise for the common good of their members. If institutions are put in place to minimise inter-ethnic conflicts, the mobilisation of ethnic groups will result in the improvement of overall well being of the nation.

Social cohesion is a major source of rebel military opportunity – ethnic and religious diversity within a country tends to reduce their ability to function (Collier and Anke 2001). The high index of ethno-linguistic fractionalisation (the probability that two randomly selected people from a given country will speak different languages) hinders rebel mobilisation and minimises wars and government overthrows. Thus, an ethnically diverse society reduces the opportunity for rebellion by limiting the recruitment pool. This aspect of ethnicity is an untapped opportunity to stabilise Africa politically and channel the huge amounts of resources wasted on internal conflicts into development of the various countries.

In the case of East Africa, the cross-border ethnic cohesion also presents a grand opportunity for regional integration. The dispersion of the Somali in Kenya, Ethiopia and Somalia, the Luhyia in Kenya and Uganda, the Maasai in Kenya and Tanzania, the Iteso in Uganda and Kenya, among others, should form a basis for integration. With cases like this of Moody Awori, a proud Luhya, holding the vice presidency in Kenya while his younger brother, Aggrey Awori, is a presidential contender in Uganda, ethnic cohesion should promote fraternalism, minimise cross-border hostilities, and hasten the pace towards a more integrated East African region. This requires recognition of cross-border traditional chiefdoms, and a guarantee of some degree of freedom to the nomadic communities to graze their livestock without the restrictions of the colonial boundaries.

Conclusion

The whole question of ethnicity and ethnic conflicts has little to do with ethnic diversity. It has everything to do with the colonial legacy of 'divide and rule', which African dictators have inherited and entrenched for their self-perpetuation. It is out of selfishness that the first rulers of independent African states entrenched ethnicity. By veiling their actions in tribal robes, the ruling elite kills two birds with one stone. First, they appeal to a tribal following, which translates into many votes, especially if such tribes are big. And second, in the event of mass dissatisfaction with their leadership, it is the ethnic group that suffers the stigma of tribalism and not the individuals.

Ethnocentrism is to a large extent a product of the failure of the political structures and institutions to tame the political elite's tendencies to seek and retain power by crooked means. This failure is inherent in the institutions of governance; most of which are too weak to provide the public with the checks and balances, needed to elicit transparency and accountability from those in power. When the people's right of political participation is constrained, causing disharmony between the citizens and the state, the former are encouraged to develop tendencies towards tribalism. This is because the state does not guarantee them a sense of security, which then they seek in the tribe. The existence of tribes, however, does not in itself cause tribalism. The main cause of tribalism is a situation in a nation whereby tribes are superficially and haphazardly amalgamated by the oppressive and constraining tendencies of the state (Kigongo 2002). These were the main features of the colonial state and continue to exist in most centralised, post-colonial states in Africa.

Widening the political spectrum of political management of the state through federalism has several positive implications. The people are afforded opportunity to elect to the state machinery a bigger number of political leaders whom they know. Thus, if the people or electorate is properly guided in electing their leaders, they are likely to elect good leaders; that is, leaders who are hardworking, development oriented, intellectually and emotionally mature, and, above all, leaders of good moral conduct. The leaders themselves, being very close to the people, would develop a sense of obligation to them to serve their interests. A good working relationship is bound to develop between the leaders and the populace, or between the state and the citizens.

In such a situation, the citizens would conceive the state not in abstract terms but as part of their life in society. Such a state of affairs is likely to forge the ethic of collective responsibility between the leaders and the populace in managing the affairs of the nation. At the same time, the society would develop a cadre of good political guardians, leaders who would have a consciousness of obligation to the citizenry. The ethic of collective responsibility and the virtue of good leadership are elements that have yet to be shaped strongly in most African countries. It would also tame dictatorial tendencies, since dictators exploit the gap between the state and citizens (Kigongo 2002).

Such decentralisation should be followed by the creation of institutions and systems of governance that recognise ethnic diversity and protect the diverse ethnic interests. If this is done, ethnicity can be a great opportunity for Africa's social, economic and political development. In my view, until and unless ethnicity is recognised as the most salient factor in the peace and stability of Africa, sustainable development will continue to elude this continent.

References

Amutabi, M.N., 1996, 'Federalism as Cure for Tribalism', in Ogot, B. A (ed.) *Ethnicity, Nationalism and Democracy in Africa*, Kisumu, Institute of Research and Postgraduate Studies, Maseno University.

Anyanwu, J.C., 2002, 'Economic and Political Causes of Civil Wars in Africa: Some Econometric Results', Economic Research Papers No. 73 (December).

Aseka, E.M., 2003, 'Politics of transition and Democracy in Africa', Fourth International Conference of the Association of Third World Studies (ATWS)— Kenya Chapter, Nairobi, Kenyatta University.

Cabral, A., 1980, *Unity and Struggle: Speeches and Writings*, London: Heinemann.

Collier, P. & Anke, H., 2001, 'Greed and Grievance in Civil War'. www.worldbank.org/research/conflict.papers.htm.

Deng, F. M., 1997, 'Ethnicity – An African Predicament', *Brookings Review*, Vol.15 No.3.

Hameso, S.Y., 1997, 'Ethnicity in Africa: Towards a Positive Approach', London: TSC.

Hasu, P., 1973, 'Race and International Politics', *Zambezia*, Vol. Three, Harare: University of Rhodesia.

Itandala, B., 1996, 'Ethnicity, Modern Nationalism and Democracy in Mainland Tanzania from 1885 to 1965', in Ogot, B. A (ed.) *Ethnicity, Nationalism and Democracy in Africa*, Institute of Research and Postgraduate Studies, Kisumu, Maseno University.

Kagwanja, P. M., 1996, 'Rethinking Democracy in Ethnically Divided Societies: A Reflection on Identity and Democratic Transition in Africa', in Ogot, B. A (ed.) *Ethnicity, Nationalism and Democracy in Africa*, Kisumu, Institute of Research and Postgraduate Studies, Maseno University.

Kenya Human Rights Commission, 1998, *Killing the Vote: State Sponsored Violence and Flawed Elections in Kenya*, Nairobi: Kenya Human Rights Commission.

Kigongo, J.K., 2002, 'Federal Governance as a Means to Effective and Meaningful Peoples' Political Participation'. www.nl.nedstatbasic.net

Kimenyi, S.M., 1989, 'Interest Groups, Transfer Seeking and Democratisation', in *The American Journal of Economics and Sociology*, Vol 48 No 3. July.

Kimenyi, S. M., 1997, 'Ethnic Diversity, Liberty and the State—The African Dilemma', The Shaftesbury Papers 12, Cheltenham: Edward Elgar Publishing Limited.

Kimenyi, S.M., 2001, *Institutions of Governance and Ethnic Conflict in Africa: A Positive View of Ethnic Governments*, Nairobi: Kenya Institute for Public Policy Research and Analysis.

Kimenyi, S.M & Mbaku, J.M., 1999, *Institutions and Collective Choice in Developing Countries: Applications of the Theory of Public Choice*, Aldershot, England: Ashgate Publishing Company.

Mazrui, A.A., 1994, 'Development in a Multi-cultural Context: Trends and Tensions', in Serageldin, I. and J. Taboroff (eds.), *Culture and Development*, Washington D.C.: World Bank.

Milazi, D., 2000, 'Ethnicity and State: Revisiting the Salience of Ethnicity in South African Politics', in Prah and Ahmed (eds.), *Africa in Transition*, Volume One, Addis Ababa: OSSREA.

Mwaruvie, J. M., 1996, 'Ethnic Imbalances in African States: A Challenge to Ideals of Nationalism and Democracy', in Ogot, B. A (ed.) Ethnicity, *Nationalism and Democracy in Africa, Kisumu*, Institute of Research and Postgraduate Studies, Maseno University.

Ngenge, T. S., 1999, *Ethnicity, Violence and Multi-party Democracy in Africa since 1989*, Ethno-Net Africa Publications. PAAA / APA.

Ogot, B. A., 1996, 'Ethnicity, Nationalism and Democracy—A kind of Historiography', in Ogot, B. A. (ed.), *Ethnicity, Nationalism and Democracy in Africa*, Kisumu, Institute of Research and Postgraduate Studies, Maseno University.

Okalany, D.H., 1996, 'Ethnicity and "Culture of Eating" in Uganda, 1962-1986', in Ogot, B. A (ed.), *Ethnicity, Nationalism and Democracy in Africa*, Kisumu, Institute of Research and Postgraduate Studies, Maseno University.

Okundiba, N., 1978, *Ethnic Politics in Nigeria*, Enugu: Fourth Dimension.

Serageldin, I., 1994, 'The Challenge of a Holistic Vision: Culture, Empowerment and the Development Paradigm', in Serageldin, I. and J. Taboroff (eds.), *Culture and Development*, Washington D.C.: World Bank.

Shivji, I. G., 2002, 'Is Might a Right in International Human Rights? Notes on the Imperialist Assault on the Right of Peoples to Self-determination', in Sifuni E. M. (ed.), *Taking Stock of Human Rights Situation in Africa*, Dar es Salaam: Faculty of Law, University of Dar es Salaam.

Simala, I.K., 1996, 'Ethnolinguistic Nationalism and Identity in Africa: Its Evolution and Implications to Nation-States', in Ogot, B. A (ed.) Ethnicity, *Nationalism and Democracy in Africa*, Kisumu: Institute of Research and Postgraduate Studies, Maseno University.

Tumin, M.M., 1964, 'Ethnic Groups', in Gould, J. and W. L. Kobs (eds.), *A Dictionary of the Social Sciences*, New York: Free Press.

World Bank, 2000, *Can Africa Claim the 21st Century?*, Washington DC.: World Bank.

Youth Agenda, 2002, *Re-creating Our Republic: The Ambitions of A Generation*, Nairobi: Youth Agenda.

6

Ethno-Centralism and Movement Politics in Uganda: New Trends and Directions in Kibaale District Elections

Mohammed Kulumba

Introduction

In the month of February 2002 during the local council elections in Kibaale, one of the most hetero-ethnic districts in Uganda, a Mukiga 'immigrant' in alliance with other ethnic groups, the Bafumbira, Baamba and Bakonzo was elected a chairperson of the district. The indigenous Banyoro rejected the results. The Banyoro who opposed the election of a Mukiga chairperson included important political and 'cultural' leaders like the members of parliament from Bunyoro and Omukama (king) of Bunyoro kingdom Solomon Gafabusa Iguru (*The New Vision*, 25 March 2002:1).[1] This was followed by bloody and destructive ethnic clashes between indigenous Banyoro and 'immigrant' ethnic groups in the district. This ethnic conflict had far reaching implications for the electoral process in the country. The conflict was unique in the sense that it was taking place at the time when it was least expected. This was especially within the context of 16 years of Movement ideology, policies and programmes and institutional building processes geared towards elimination of ethnic-based conflict in Uganda. The Movement Political System under which Uganda has been governed since 1986[2] assumes every citizen to be a member regardless of political party affiliation or ideology. In addition, elections both for local and national for different political posts are conducted on the basis of individual merit. In addition political party activities are limited to their headquarters. They are not allowed to operate nationally or to field candidates during local or national elections while the Movement government is in power.[3] According to 1995 Republican Constitution of Uganda, which has been dubbed a 'Movement government constitution' by some scholars, the system can be changed only through a referendum. Since its promulgation, a referendum was held once, in March 2001. The Movement won by 70 percent (The Uganda Electoral Commission Report, March 2001 Referendum).

Rupesinghe (1989: back cover page) observed in the early days of the Movement government that:

> 'There is a new mood in Uganda. There is a determination to break out of the bitter history of internal conflict. Uganda gives hope to all those other areas of the world where violence has become endemic such as Ulster, Lebanon and Sri Lanka'.[4]

Syahuka-Muhindo (1993:276) makes a pertinent contention, which is relevant to our analysis of ethnic conflict in Kibaale district. He argues that::

> Historical grievances, often articulated through ethnic explosions, build up over a long period of time. When the explosions take place and necessitate probing, ethnic violence rather than the root causes of the problem become the central focus of state appointed commissions and academicians. Attempts, which are sometimes frantic, are made to resolve the problem. This is done without a concrete understanding of the historical causes.[5]

We therefore attempt to build our understanding and interpretation of the ethnic conflict in Kibaale by analysing the history, contradictions within the Movement ideology, politics, policies and practice, and bringing out the link between them and the conflict in Kibaale. The conflict in Kibaale offers a perfect model for analysis in terms of relationships between ethnocentrism and electoral processes under the Movement ideology and practice. The working thesis for this chapter is that Kibaale conflict was a result of the contradictions between the theory, policies and practice of the Movement politics by Movement government.

It appears that there is a divergence between the Movement government ideology, policies and practice, in the sense that they are implemented to the extent that they legitimise the Movement government. Put differently, even if the ideology, policy or programme or any institutional framework is in place and relevant towards elimination of conflict and ensures democratic practice and social order, it will not be implemented as long as it would undermine continued existence of Movement government.

Conceptual Issues: Ethnicity and Conflict

Ethnicity and Conflict

The fact that post-independence Africa is prone to conflict and that many of these are linked to ethnicity has generated massive literature. The literature referred to in this section is from various scholars and researchers, both local and international, on levels of conflict in Africa. In one such endeavour, Chukwu (2000:141) defines an ethnic group as:

a distinct category of people within a society, who are bound together by certain cultural features that differentiate them from other groups in the same society. The term 'ethnic group' is sometimes used interchangeably with 'tribal' groups. In several African states, some of the groups, which presently conceive themselves as ethnic groups, were previously made up of some antagonistic units without a definite solidifying ethnic base. Ethnicity is a clear fact in human experience. Everywhere around the globe, people identify themselves with different ethnic groups. It is the significance which a group accords to ethnicity in their worldly quest for values that makes it appear as a source of conflict particularly in some African countries'.[6]

Chukwu's definition leaves some theoretical and empirical gaps that require some explanation. For example, if everywhere around the globe, people identify themselves with different ethnic groups, why is it that in some polities, these groups coexist in harmony and are actually useful in the establishment of social order of these societies? Why is it that in other societies there is violent ethnic conflict? Is it really correct to assert that it is the significance, which a group accords to ethnicity in their worldly quest for values that makes it appear as a source of conflict particularly in Africa? Chukwu does point out specifically, that according to historical evidence, some of the ethnic groups that appear now to be solid, cohesive and important political actors within their societies experienced much conflict and antagonism. The pertinent question one may ask is; why are they so cohesive and powerful now to the extent that their actions lead to a breakdown of order in society?

Kayunga (1995:242) explains that historical factors and African leaders' styles in politics are important in understanding contemporary ethnicity in Africa. The historical factors include:

> The failure of colonialism to destroy pre-capitalist social formations, which has led to an amorphous class structure in Africa. Because of the amorphousness of the social classes in Africa, ethnicity has offered a much more convenient basis for political and social organization. This in turn has led to the reinforced ethnic solidarity at the expense of class consciousness, especially at the time of economic crisis... due to the absence of a clear social base on which to graft their power, a number of African leaders adopted a patron-client relationship in their leadership styles. The major tendency in this leadership style, or ethno-clientism, was the provision of selective access to political offices and national resources.

Kayunga's theoretical discourse clarifies important issues in relation to ethnic conflict in Africa, but at the same time raises questions that remain unanswered. For example, if the current ethnicity can be explained in terms of the undemocratic nature of the post-colonial state, why would the response to it be inter-ethnic violence? There are, to be sure, states in Africa where ethnicity does not play a major role. In a country like Tanzania with many ethnic groupings, there has for a long time been relatively peaceful co-existence among these groups.

The plausible explanation is that in Tanzania, the Chama Cha Mapinduzi political party (CCM) initiated mechanisms that transformed the post-colonial state. These mechanisms included universal education and village-ization during Tanzania's experiment with African socialism.

Secondly, why is it that many post independence African leaders have failed to destroy pre-capitalist social formations? Isn't it true that their continued existence is in their interest? This, in particular when they undermine institutions, policies and mechanisms that can lead to their elimination? If ethnic groups can indeed be an effective means for social order as A. R. Nsibambi contends (1997:54), then how can we avoid situations where they turn into vehicles for conflict and violence?

Finally, Kayunga, Chukwu or Nsibambi do not address contemporary practice in Africa where political actors within a state, create, organise and finance previously dormant and unconscious ethnic groups for political action that favours their continued overstay in power. This phenomenon is common especially towards elections. Indeed it is believed to be responsible for most of the contemporary election violence in Africa.

Juma (2002:32), appears to offer a more convincing explanation as to why African leaders, and in particular the Movement government use the state to reconstruct, organise and facilitate previously dormant and unconscious ethnic groups for political action. He contextualises this phenomenon as a quest for political legitimacy and consolidation of power in the case of regimes with a narrow social base. For example, he argues that in the case of Movement government in Uganda:

> When it suits him, President Museveni has not hesitated to deploy sectarianism in ethnicity or religion, to retain power. He has used these sectarian mechanisms as long as they fit into his strategy for retaining power at all costs. He gives the example of the restoration of Buganda Monarchy prior to Constituency Assembly (CA) elections and the promise to mainly Baganda Catholic clergy, shortly before the 12 March 2001 Presidential elections, that a Muganda Catholic would succeed him as revealing the President's agenda for political power and legitimacy.

For that matter it would be wishful thinking to expect post-colonial African leaders to institute and support mechanisms towards the elimination of the negative dimensions of ethnic consciousness. This is indeed difficult when such consciousness is in their political interest. This confirms Bayatt's contention (1993:47) that, '... contemporary ethnic groups, far from being the links between post-colonial state and its historical background, are often of recent creation'. He adds that ethnicity can also be a channel through which redistribution is demanded as well as being a means of accumulation. In other words, ethnic conflict is least expected in a society where there are no government-induced political, social and economic inequalities.

We need for our part to explore the link if any between the Movement government sectarianism and the Kibaale ethnic conflict which we do in this chapter.

Movement Debates and Electoral Process

The Movement and the electoral process have generated a lot of debates and criticisms from scholars and political actors regarding its politics and practice. The debates and criticisms fall mainly under two broad categories, the supporters and opposers of Movement canons and practices. Kabwegere (2000:91) bases his support on the reality that: 'Since 1986, elections in Uganda have become popular and frequent occurrence. Ugandans have had a chain of major elections of 1987, 1989 and 1992, the National Resistance Council (NRC) elections of 1989, the CA elections of 1994, the Presidential and Parliamentary elections of 1996, and the Local Council (LC) elections of 1998.'

Indeed he rightly points out that 'elections legitimise positions of those in possession of power'. He however fails to point to the phenomenon where the incumbent power holders engineer the electoral process when it seems that the election results would not confer them with the needed legitimacy. Was this the scenario during the Kibaale district elections?

According to Mukwaya (2001:64), the Movementocratic governance debate emphasises the failures of western democracy and multiparty pluralism to appreciate African conditions and peoples. It is argued that the:

> Movement as a home-grown African type of democratic governance is a must in the drive towards finding Africa's solutions to Africa's problems. Movementocracy asserts that the concepts of democracy and good governance are universal and therefore they need to strictly embrace the African conditions.[7]

We are not going to enter the debate over the 'Africanness' of the Movement or why it has succeeded in governing the country for almost twenty years. This has been done elsewhere (Kulumba 2001:3).[8]

Mujaju (1996:13) dismisses the Movement thesis that political parties would not be able to hold nations together in the Third World countries. He argues that 'India, the second largest peasant nation (China is first), is held together by the Congress party. Undoubtedly, without the Congress party, India could very easily have broken apart many years ago'. Therefore, for him, instead of governing the people according to outmoded Marxist concepts, the people should be given their legitimate rights to promote their parties or form new ones. He concludes that the real intention of NRM is not to improve things but to monopolise power.[9] Mujaju advances empirical and theoretical evidence about the Movement ideology, politics and practice. We examine whether the ethnic conflict in Kibaale is linked to a Movement intention to monopolise power in the subsequent sections of this chapter.

According to Oloka-Onyango (2000:5):

The theory and practice of Movement and one party states appear to have more similarities than differences. The 'No-Party' Movement political system is neither unique nor is it an exemplary expression of the democratic ideal. The Movement is nothing more than the guided democracy of the old (one party system) in which political expression is both dictated and suppressed by the ruling political organization of the day. But since by the 1980s, One- Partyism had fallen into disrepute, it was conveniently repackaged as Movement to lend it credibility both within and outside Uganda. Indeed the movement has not managed to eliminate the divisions brought about by ethnicity and religion attributed to the multiparty political system in the 16 (20) years of governing the country.[10]

Juma (2000:5) points out the paradox of ethnic conflict in a Movement and in a more open political system. He counsels that 'the best way to manage ethnic conflict and ethnic consciousness is more and not less democratisation'. He argues that ethnicity in Uganda can be managed mainly in two ways. First, the answer to the dilemma posed by ethnicity lies in structural changes that address political, social and economic inequity and imbalances in power. Second, through democratisation, to build democratic institutions for peaceful transfer of power and tolerance of alternative political views in society. He concludes by asserting that no ethnically plural society is likely to avoid using the processes of democratisation and power sharing in the long run if it is to enjoy political stability and acceptable level of social cohesion.[11]

It has also been observed that the worst students of the Movement have been its founders/promoters. They follow policies and take actions that are contrary to Movement principles and values. This is mainly at the practical level. In previous local and national elections, the Movement has nominated, supported and financed candidates, thus contravening the Movement's own principle of individual merit. There has also been the categorisation of members of the Movement as 'historicals', 'freshers', 'hardliners' and 'moderates' which is unconstitutional (Kulumba, ibid:5).[12] We need to find out for example whether such Movement practice was reproduced in Kibaale district.

The Electoral Issues

One of the landmarks under Movement governance as we have noted, has been the holding of regular elections both at the local administrations and national levels in Uganda since 1986. The major context of these elections has been that earlier electoral processes were reinforced by the use of the gun. In addition, according to Makara et al (1996:1):

Ugandan political elites vying for political offices have confused and divided the electorate along ethnic or religious ground or both. Politics in Uganda since independence in 1962, has been marked by intrigue, manipulation, violence, force, intimidation and outright violation of human rights. In short, democratic governance has eluded Uganda since independence and the country has been steered through crises.

These tendencies referred to by Makara et al were greatly reduced during Movement-organised elections (Kulumba 2001: 5). However as Parekh (1993:171) states, that:

> In an ethnically and religiously diverse society lacking shared values, or in a society unused to discussing its differences in public and articulating in neat ideological rigidities, elections release powerful aggressive impulses and channel them into dangerous and unconstitutional directions. Such societies might be better off sticking to, or evolving consensual and less polarized ways of selecting their governments and conducting their affairs.

Does this contention also apply to elections in Uganda? The phenomenon, which Parekh is articulating, has been manifested in Movement elections in many ways. For example, in an earlier parliamentary election the contest was between, among others, different religious groups. In Kyagenyi sub-county, Sheema county, Bushenyi district, elections were postponed for months until the hot religious/party contest was defused' (Kabwegere 2000:97). This appears to confirm Oloka-Onyango's assertion (1989:478) that 'provided social-economic and political realities in Uganda perpetuate fundamental inequalities and injustices, the law (institutions and elections) by itself, can do little to implement a regime of genuine grass root democracy'. This raises several questions. For example, was it the Movement failure in addressing inequalities and injustices in relation to agrarian questions in Kibaale that sparked off ethnic conflict? Can we interpret ethnic conflict in Kibaale as a rural protest against agrarian questions?

Kabwegere points out the dilemma of democracy in a country like Uganda. He argues that:

> Establishing democracy in a Third World country like Uganda is not simply about building institutions germane to democracy; it is not simply a question of having parties and elections and parliament. It is a question of social transformation of proportions that can validly be called a social revolution. It must involve the education of masses to be democratic in thought, belief and actions; the masses must appreciate what it means to be undemocratic and its implications for the individual and for society. Democracy must not only be seen in artifacts, but also in values so that

the people can press for its practice, and can correct its mistakes and nature its growth.

We agree with Kabwegere's contention. The question we are asking however is, what has been the impact of the Movement political programmes intentions to educate the masses so as to lead to a social transformation of Uganda society? Can we associate the failure of these programmes with the Movement's politics? Where do we place the theory, politics and practice of the Movement within the context of ethnic conflict in Kibaale district?

Context of Ethnic Conflict in Kibaale District

A history of Kibaale ethnic conflict

Ethnic conflict in Kibaale is linked to the history of several waves of migrations dating back to the 19th Century. The first was a result of Omukama (king) Kabalega's succession wars of 1852 and 1869. These drove people out of southern part of Bunyoro kingdom to this region. The second was caused by Bunyoro's wars against her neighbours, conquering some and subjugating others to tributary status. Indeed Bunyoro's early history is one of military expansion until the middle of the 19th Century (Kiwanuka 1991:23).

Another wave is attributed to British wars of 1893–1899, assisted by Buganda, that resulted in the collapse of Bunyoro-Kitara Kingdom and the formation of Toro kingdom among others by Kaboyo. Although the Bamba and Bakonzo in the former Bunyoro-Kitara kingdom initially assisted in the formation of Toro kingdom, they were subsequently alienated by Kaboyo. Some of the Bamba and Bakonzo migrated from Burahya and Bunyangabo counties to Buyaga and Bugaingaizi in Kibaale district. Others settled in the areas around Lake Kagadi in Masindi district (Syahuka-Muhindo 1993:289). If Bunyoro and Kibaale in particular had experienced several waves of migrations before, why then didn't the earlier migrations lead to ethnic conflict like that seen in the 2002 local council elections in Kibaale district, Bunyoro kingdom? One may be tempted to argue that these migrations of Bamba, Bakonzo and other settlers constituted only 23 percent of the total population in Bunyoro kingdom (1959 Census). Therefore they were no threat to the indigenous Banyoro, who formed about 77 percent of the kingdom's population. This argument in our view misses the point. To understand the different response of indigenous Banyoro to similar situation of migrants, one needs to focus on concrete objectives of various waves of migration. This is in addition to the different forms of rule in Bunyoro during these varying periods. The explanation partly lay in the recent migration to Kibaale district.

The recent migrants to Kibaale district can be divided in two categories. According to Nuwagaba (2002:6), the first were mainly Bakiga and Bafumbira from over-populated districts of Kabaale and Bushenyi. They came through deliberate government resettlement schemes. The first one was carried out in the 1970s and the second in the 1990s. Both schemes were involuntary. The Bakiga and Bafumbira were given two options by the government: 'migration to Kibaale and in particular Bugaigaizi county where each family was given ten acres of land, or starve in their over-populated home districts'.

The second recent movement of migrants to Kibaale took place in 1992. This one too was involuntary. It affected the Bakiga and Bafumbira who had illegally settled in the Mpokya Forest Reserve in Kabarole district. The Mpokya Forest Game Reserve extends partly to Kibaale district. These new Bakiga and Bafumbira immigrants were settled in Bugaigaizi County, in the Northern part of Kibaale district.

Another important historical dimension to Kibaale ethnic conflict is the reality that the district of Kibaale occupies the land area that constitutes part of what is known as the 'lost counties' of Bunyoro kingdom. Towards the end of the 19th Century, all the Bunyoro territory south of the river Kafu was transferred to Buganda, and the Buganda Agreement of 1900 confirmed the transfer. Contrary to the general belief in most of the literature, the lost counties were not given to Buganda by the British as a reward for her efforts in the war efforts against Bunyoro. Indeed according to Roberts (1962:197), 'the annexation of the lost counties of Bunyoro while due in part to a number of misunderstandings, was originally undertaken by the British for primarily military reasons, and was confirmed chiefly in order to avoid provoking barely concealed religious dissension'.

Besides these debates the 'lost counties' have reproduced several implications past and recent. First, between 1900 and 1902, hundreds of Banyoro migrated from this area to escape the rule of Baganda chiefs who treated them somewhat like serfs (Low and Pratt 1960:55). One outcome of this was the Nyangire revolt in Bunyoro, protest against British imposition of Baganda chiefs (Jorgensen 1981:61). In effect the event left behind a large and unoccupied territory.

Second, apart from political implications, there was also the agrarian question. The land in Kibaale was partitioned under Buganda Agreement of 1900, that introduced Milo land tenure system, introduced by the colonial state, especially in Buganda kingdom. The tenure which is still operating in Uganda involves the holding of registered land in perpetuity while at the same time allowing the bona fide occupant to carry out developments on the land. Under the original Mailo land tenure system, land was divided between the Kabaka (king), chiefs, and the colonial state (Low and Pratt 1960:107). Although Bunyoro tried several times, from as early as 1912, to recover these counties (land) from Buganda, she only succeeded in 1964 when a referendum was held over the issue. According to Kiapi (1989:95); 'Two of the disputed counties, Buyaga and Bugangaizi, voted for their re-union with Bunyoro, and parliament passed the necessary Bill for their transfer'. Kiapi aptly notes that this was a clear case where a constitution was used as a mediator in internal conflict. The important question in our case is; why didn't the Movement government use the 1995 constitution to mediate in the Kibaale ethnic conflict?

It is worth noting that while the 1964 Bill transferred the two counties to Bunyoro, land rights remained with the original Baganda allotee under the 1900 Buganda Agreement.

Finally, we should note that the Bamba and Bakonzo had migrated much earlier to Bunyoro through the first wave of migrants, and had coexisted with Banyoro without any problem.

Also, as we have noted in this chapter, the ethnic conflict between Banyoro on the one hand and Bamba, Bakonzo, Bakiga and Bafumbira on the other, took place during the Kibaale district elections in 2002. This was a period of more than ten decades after the last involuntary settlement of Bakiga in Kibaale district.

At the same time it is also important to note that while the first wave of immigrants, the Bakonjo and Bamba, could be rightly categorised as refugees running away from impossible circumstances, the recent immigrants, the Bakiga and Bafumbira, came simply for land. Therefore there was bound to be conflict over agrarian questions in Kibaale. What was the impact of all these developments for the area?

We attempt to respond to this question and others raised in the chapter by analysing three issues: land question, restoration of 'cultural' monarchy, and Movement local council electoral process in Kibaale.

Land Question and Kibaale Conflict

Nuwagaba (2002:3) and other scholars have attributed ethnic conflict in Kibaale to the land question, in particular Buganda Mailo land system.[13] His central thesis is that Kibaale ethnic conflict comprises an issue regarding land management, which itself is as a result of the failure by successive Ugandan governments to adequately resolve land tenure and management systems in Kibaale. In particular, the Bunyoro kingdom 'lost counties' of Buyaga and Bugangaizi which are at the centre of contention in the Kibaale crisis.

In contrast to Nuwagaba thesis, we argue that the role of Mailo land system or the land question merely is intended to mask the concrete realities behind the conflict. We contend that at the centre of ethnic conflict in Kibaale is the nature of politics and practice of the Movement government. To this extent, we are in agreement with Mahmood Mamdani's assertion (1996:185), namely that '... it would make more sense to speak of the making of an ethnicity' by the state or the major political actors of the time. The Mailo land tenure system has been in existence in Buganda and in the 'lost counties' since it was introduced by the colonial state in 1900. One may be tempted to ask why it is only now that the dynamics of the Mailo land tenure and its politics come into play? Secondly, why didn't ethnic conflict take place in other 'lost counties'?[14] The 'lost counties' historically included, in addition to Buyaga and Bugangaizi in Kibaale district, also Rugojo (North Ssingo), Buruli, and Buyaga in Bugerere (Karugire 1987:223).

There is evidence that people and peasants in particular have lived on the Mailo land and carried out developments without any threat from 'present' and/ or 'absentee' landlords. According to Low and Pratt, (1960:143):

> The new system (Mailo), moreover, provided capital for Africans earlier than in many other places in Africa, and certainly earlier than anywhere else in Uganda. With the unrestricted right to buy ...enclosed in the land settlement, went too the creation of attainable economic incentives for peasants; while the land settlement also allowed for greater capital accumulation... economic stimuli were thus provided, and notable economic progress made possible.

If Banyoro ethnic consciousness centred around Mailo land tenure, they had an opportunity to address this issue once and for all, under the Land Reform Decree of 1975. This decree turned all the land in Uganda into public land to be administered by the Uganda Land Commission in accordance with the Public Land Act (Nsibambi 1989:224). Thus the Banyoro, if they had so wished, could have applied for the land in Kibaale through the Uganda Land Commission. But they did not. Although as Nsibambi (ibid) argues, 'Amin's regime was too often anarchic and that Amin did not care about land tangles', the regime is known to have implemented public policies especially those that appeared to have popular support. The land in Kibaale was certainly not one of them.

The only notable land conflict in Buganda was The Bataka (clan heads) uprising against the colonial state for allocating their ancestral land to the Kabaka (king) of Buganda and his chiefs.[15] According to Mamdani (1976:123), 'In creating a class of landed gentry, the 1900 Agreement had undermined the position of... the traditional Bataka (the clan heads who controlled ancestral lands, counted in terms of villages)'. This conflict was clearly not about the antagonistic relationship between landlords and peasants, but over the colonial land policy. By taking away land from the Bataka, the colonial state succeeded in eroding their political power base in Buganda, a move that they obviously resisted.

Another important dimension to the Mailo land tenure system in Buganda in contrast to Bunyoro is that immigrant peasants came and they continue to come and stay at will. Indeed according to Jorgensen, (1981:61), 'By the very success of African commercial production, Southern Uganda (Buganda) attracted migrant labourers (peasants) from.. Rwanda-Burundi and Southern Sudan'. The majority were assimilated into the Baganda cultural system and acquired land for peasant agriculture.

In contrast with Bunyoro for example, '... despite the abolition of rent and tribute, landlords retained many prerogatives: high social status, the power of eviction and the right to prohibit tenants from erecting permanent structures (Dunbar 1965:143). We must point out that these were the main features of the land tenure system in Bunyoro Kingdom. Even the cultivation of perennial crops by a peasant was sufficient cause for eviction (Dunbar *ibid*: 141). Is the conflict in Kibaale a demand by Banyoro for a return of this Bunyoro 'traditional' land tenure system?

In comparison with Buganda, 'the 1928 Busuulu and Evujjo law fixed the rent and tribute payable to the Mailo land owner by a plot holder, limiting the freedom of the Mailo owner to evict tenants. The Mailo land system created a land owning class and a land market, because land was henceforth a commodity which could be sold and mortgaged' (Nsibambi 1989:223). This can be done freely regardless of one's ethnic identity. Indeed, this has contributed to the development of commercial farming in areas like Kawolo. This is impossible in the north and southwestern parts of the country where landholding is based on communal rights. For example, Major General Salim Saleh, a brother to President Yoweri Museveni from southwestern Uganda could not buy land in Acholi in the North for his Poverty Alleviation Projects. He was not qualified to own land in this part of the country where land holding is communal. To this extent, Mailo land appears to be more developmental, especially to the Movement government policy of 'Modernising Agriculture in the country'. This in our view is a healthy development that can provide employment to people in the rural areas instead of encouraging entrenchment of a peasantry through poorly planned internal settlement schemes in the countryside. Salim Saleh's case is similar to the Bakiga, Bafumbira, Bamba and Bakozo immigrants in Kibaale district.

The only notable threat to bona fide occupants on Mailo land came mainly from land speculators and land grabbers. Such persons obtained large chunks of land in anticipation of profits. Most of them used to be politicians or people with political connections. They were able to get 'political loans' mainly from Uganda Commercial Bank (UCB). The Rwandan President, Paul Kagame for example, bought many acres of land in Mubende (Buganda) under this scheme. He was able to repay the UCB loan after the Rwandan Patriotic Front's capture of state power in 1994. Their activities have however been limited by the privatisation of the banking sector.

At another level, to associate Kibaale ethnic conflict with lost counties and the assertion that the 1964 referendum returned the counties to Bunyoro, while the land ownership remained in Buganda, is false. We noted that the relationship between landlords and bona fide occupants under the Mailo land system has never been antagonistic. Indeed we have not witnessed any Banyoro uprising against Baganda 'absentee' landlords in Bunyoro. Additionally, right from the colonial period to date, Buganda's contentious issues have always been presented in a well coordinated and organised form to the holders of state power variously as Buganda we'yimiridde (our position) and or Ebyaffe (our things/demands).[16] Buganda for example, demanded a federal arrangement during the Lancaster Independence Conference and in 1994 constitutional-making debates in the Constituent Assembly. In the former she was granted a semi-federal arrangement, while in the latter, districts in Buganda were deemed to have cooperated after the coming into force of the 1995 Constitution (see the 1962 and 1995 Uganda Constitutions).

The land in the lost counties ceased to be part of Buganda's demands after the 1964 referendum, which returned them to Bunyoro. We are not suggesting that Buganda assented to the return of the counties. The point is that without Buganda's backing as an entity, the lost counties issue subsided and it was left to individual Baganda landlords. Even then, there has never been any Muganda landlord with land in Kibaale who threatened bona fide occupants by selling land or any other form of eviction. The Kibaale ethnic conflict therefore has no direct link with them.

In 1998, the NRM government enacted a Land Act. The Act's objective was to provide for tenure, ownership and management of land in Uganda. The Act also stipulates that all land in Uganda shall rest in the citizens of Uganda and shall be owned in accordance with the following land tenure systems: (i) Customary (ii) Freehold (iii) Mailo (iv) Leasehold.

In addition, the Act provides for the establishment of District, Sub-county and Urban Land Tribunals. We have already noted that land in Kibaale is under Mailo tenure and occupied under Rights recognised by the constitution and the 1998 Land Act. However, four years after enactment of this Act, it has not been implemented. If the Act had been operational, land issues or conflict would have been handled by Land Tribunals provided for under the Act. Since the Movement has had no political will and interests to ensure its implementation, it has largely remained dormant.

Finally, the Movement government in the midst of ethnic conflict in Kibaale, appointed a cabinet committee to investigate the matter (*The New Vision*, 17 April, 2002:19).[17] The committee made the following recommendations:

i)   The further influx of immigrants into Kibaale district be halted;
ii)   Illegal immigrants to be resettled in alternative places;
iii)   The 1998 Land Act to be implemented;
iv)   President Museveni to intervene; and
v)   Government to formulate a resettlement policy.

The government accepted all these recommendations. The exception was the Land Act and the resettlement policy. It was indeed absurd for a government that prides itself in the democratisation of the country to deny citizens their constitutional rights to settle anywhere in Uganda. The issue is not the absence of policies or institutional frameworks, but rather the lack of Movement interest.

Restoration of the Bunyoro 'Cultural' Monarchy and Resistance Councils (RCs)

It is our contention that the roots of the contemporary ethnic conflict in Kibaale lay in the contradictions within the Movement principles, politics and practice in a number of ways. One of them is the restoration of 'Traditional Leaders' in the governance (cultural) of the country. When the Movement government took over power in 1986, it was only the Baganda who were notable for their demand for the restoration of Ebyaffe. 'Ebyaffe' is a Luganda concept that embodies the Bugandan struggles to restore the Buganda kingdom, including the assets that were confiscated in 1966 by UPC government. Indeed, if there had been no demand for the revival of the Buganda monarchy, there probably would have been no-one particularly concerned with Bunyoro, Toro or Bunyoro kingdoms (Doornbos and Mwesigye 1997:64).[18]

However, the Traditional Leaders Act passed in 1994, and Chapter 16 of the 1995 Constitution, that regulates the Institutions of Traditional or Cultural Leaders, not only restored Buganda's traditional institutions, but also allowed any other area that wished to have them go ahead. Article 246 contains provisions that have made the existence of traditional leaders not only precarious, but also tend to bring them into dispute with political actors both local and national. These provisions include the following:

i) A traditional leader or cultural leader shall enjoy such privileges and benefits as may be conferred by the government and local government, or as the leader may be entitled to under culture, custom and tradition.

ii) Subject to the clause above, no person shall be compelled to pay allegiance or contribute to the cost of maintaining a traditional leader.

iii) A person shall not, while remaining a traditional leader or cultural leader, join or participate in partisan politics.

iv) Any custom, practice, usage or tradition relating to a traditional or cultural leader, which detracts from the rights of any person, as guaranteed by this constitution, shall be taken to be prohibited.

v) For the avoidance of any doubt, the institution of traditional leader existing immediately before the coming into force of this Constitution shall be taken to exist in accordance with the provisions of this Constitution.

The Bunyoro Kingdom was one that was presumed to have existed and to have been legalised by the coming into force of 1995 constitution. However, the Bunyoro monarchy was restored at a time when the area had undergone fundamental political and social-economic changes. For example, the Bakiga, Baamba, Bakonzo and Bafumbira immigrants had not only grown in terms of population, but also they had become economically powerful in relative terms. Therefore, when the Movement government policy allowed the restoration of Bunyoro monarchy without independent sources of revenue and left its sustainability to the will of subjects, there were bound to be ethnic tensions. This is especially so where the economically powerful residents were not 'citizens' of the Bunyoro monarchy, and yet they were assumed by the Constitution to be willing to give financial privileges and benefits to the monarchy. Moreover, going by their tradition they have no attachment and values to any monarchical institution.

The presence of economically powerful acephalous ethnic groups in Bunyoro could have been inconsequential. After all, the restored Buganda monarchy regarded as being a model for traditional institutions in many ways has sustained itself financially from Baganda, non-Baganda, and even non-citizens of Uganda. However in the case of Bunyoro, the monarchy was not as cherished and valued even among the indigenous Banyoro. This could be attributed to the fact that although the Banyoro traditional clan system is akin to that of Baganda, its hierarchical arrangement is not as strong as in Buganda. In Buganda, every Muganda has a natural attachment to the monarchy in contrast to Bunyoro. This is well corroborated by Richards (1960:100), who observes that:

> Every Nyoro belongs to one of 150 clans, each of which is associated with a particular ritual avoidance object (Muziro). These clans never form corporate units and, in Bunyoro at least, there is nothing corresponding to the clan councils found in neighbouring kingdom (Buganda).

Thus, in Bunyoro the monarchy's legitimacy is not based on Banyoro's 'cherished cultural values' but on blood relationship of the ruling Babito dynasties. They are a few. Indeed, the traditional Bunyoro state centred around the personality of Omukama (King), and not clan leaders down to the ordinary Munyoro.

Secondly, the restoration of a cultural monarchy in Bunyoro brought forward the issue of citizen and subject with all its consequences in a heterogeneous district like Kibaale. As we noted, there had been earlier waves of migration by Bamba and Bakonzo to Bunyoro kingdom and Kibaale district in particular. These however did not give birth to ethnic conflict. The explanation for this fact lies in the form of the monarchy at the time. The king did not only rule, but governed as well. Thus all subjects, whether immigrants or indigenous, were expected to be loyal and to pay tributes to the monarchy. This was also true in 1964 during Omukama's brief rule when the 'lost counties', Buyaga and Bugaingaizi in Kibaale district, were returned to Bunyoro kingdom before the abolition of kingdoms in 1967.

The restoration of a cultural monarchy thus divided Bunyoro (Kibaale) into subjects and citizens of Kibaale district. The former had no cultural rights to stay and therefore had to leave. It is therefore clear that the loss of the King's political power to force compliance of subjects, and in its place a powerless cultural monarchy, is partly responsible for ethnic conflict in Kibaale district. Given the changed circumstances, a significant section of Banyoro was not anxious about restoration. In fact, many Banyoro and immigrants were simply waiting for an opportune moment to resist the monarchy, which presented itself in contested district local council elections.

Thirdly, restoration of the traditional institution as a 'cultural' and not a political entity made the monarchy much more exposed and vulnerable. The cultural monarchy could not enforce rules and norms. That is why the Omukama of Bunyoro, Solomon Iguru, was at the forefront in mobilising the Banyoro against the elected Mukiga chairman of Kibaale district. According to *The Monitor Newspaper*, (9 April 2002), the Omukama is alleged to have told the Banyoro that 'immigrants are causing a lot of problems in his kingdom. They come when they are poor, with no land and proceed to amass wealth. I am appealing to the Movement government to protect the Banyoro against such injustices'.

It is clear that the king's action did not only exacerbate ethnic hatred and tensions, but it was also unconstitutional. It violated the constitutional provisions which bar traditional leaders from participating in partisan politics. On the other hand, through his actions, the king was denying a significant section of his community, the Bakiga, Baamba, Bakonzo and Bafumbira, their inalienable right to elect their leaders. But because the Movement government was not ready to antagonise the Banyoro and needed their support for political legitimacy, there was no sense and urgency in using the constitution as a mediator in the conflict.

We should also note that the once famous kingdom of Ankole has not been restored. Though there is a minority group among Banyankole who would like to see a return of their traditional institution, the majority do not. The Movement government went to the extent of nullifying the coronation of the heir to the throne, John Barigye in 1993 (Doornbos and Mwesigye 1997:72). This was in the absence of any contestation regarding his legitimacy to the throne, unlike Bunyoro traditional leadership, which was resolved in court. One of the arguments of those who are against restoration is that Ankole kingship was oppressive in the past and that only a section of Banyankole (Bahima) benefited from it. The reality however appears to be the fear of the Movement to antagonise the support of the majority who oppose the restoration. This raises the question regarding minority rights of those that support restoration. Our view is that regardless of the dynamism of the monarchy in Ankole, such action by NRM is antithetical to the process of institution building in the country. In any case, if a monarchy was unpopular in the past and alienated some social groups, it is wrong to assume that it would follow the same policies in case it was restored.

For example, in the past, Buganda monarchy excluded Catholics and Muslims from the main administrative hierarchy of the kingdom. They were limited to low level ministerial posts and could not aspire to be appointed to the prestigious Katikiroship (Prime Minister) of Buganda. Indeed the alienation of the Catholics was responsible for the formation of Democratic Party (DP) in the early

1950s to fight against Catholic marginalisation by Buganda kingdom. However, Kabaka Mutebi has since the restoration of the Buganda monarchy appointed a Catholic Katikiro. His action has to a great extent addressed that historic Catholic grievance against the Buganda monarchy. We believe Prince Barigye could have done the same with the Banyankole who felt that the institution had been oppressive in the past. Indeed he had proceeded by appointing a Prime Minister who was from the Biiru ethnic group, alleged to have been oppressed in the past. However, he was denied this opportunity by the Movement politics when his coronation was nullified. The reality of human society is that institutions die naturally once they cease to be useful, unless they are propelled by dictatorial tendencies. For this reason, the survival of cultural institutions will have to depend on their capacity to innovate useful ways for their communities. This will, among other things, ensure their independence particularly from a predatory government.

Movement Local Council Electoral Process in Kibaale

Before the Movement government's capture of state power in 1986, local government administration in Uganda enjoyed a unitary relationship with the central government. For example, according to the 1967 constitution, even a simple bye-law proposed by the lowest local unit had to be approved by the central government Minister of Local Government. The introduction of Resistance Council Committees (RCs), which later came to be known as Local Councils (LCs), thus changed a centralised element in the local government system to a decentralised one. Decentralisation, which is the transfer of powers, functions and responsibilities from the centre to lower levels of government, began in earnest in 1993 when the enabling legislation was passed. Although decentralisation was undertaken as an experiment in 13 districts, by 1995 all districts had been granted decentralised powers and functions.

Decentralisation was further enshrined in the 1995 constitution. The following provisions and principles, which regulate the decentralisation policy in Uganda and incorporated in the constitution, are important for our analysis. They include:

i) The principle that local government shall be based on democratically elected councils on the basis of universal adult suffrage;

ii) A local government shall be based on a council, which shall be the highest political authority within its area of jurisdiction;

iii) There shall be a District Chairperson who shall be a political head of the district who is elected by universal adult suffrage through a secret ballot;

iv) The District Chairperson or Speaker of a district council may be removed from office by the council by resolutions supported by the votes of not less than two-thirds of all members of the council;

v) The president may, with the approval of two-thirds of all the members of parliament, assume the executive and legislative powers of any district.

The decentralisation policy, besides the Movement politics and practice, could be said to be one of the major contributions to the democratisation of Uganda. However, this policy has been manipulated for selfish political interests. The Kibaale conflict puts this observation into focus in a number of ways. First, although it is clear from the constitutional provisions that the election of a chairperson must be carried out democratically through universal adult suffrage, this was not the case in Kibaale. The chairperson-elect who won, through what may be considered a democratic process, was denied opportunity to lead. Instead, the Movement government initiated a process where purported leaders of Banyoro (not elected) and members of Immigrant Association (Bafurikyi/immigrants) handpicked a 'compromise candidate' to replace a democratically elected chairperson. This act in many ways undermined the policy of decentralisation initiated by the Movement government. This episode confirms Mamdani's observation (1996:216) in relation to the Movement politics; 'As direct elections broadened oppositional access to rural constituencies, the NRM (Movement) found it difficult to hold firm the social alliance of peasants and migrants that it had forged during the guerrilla struggle'. A dilemma does indeed arise with the transfer of political and administrative power to local councils through decentralisation in a territory where a cultural monarchy exists. One wonders why Kibaale district has not adopted the political power sharing arrangement for district posts. This arrangement has solved ethnic tensions between Basoga and migrant ethnic groups in Bugiri district, Busoga kingdom. According to Makiika (2002:15): '... the Basamia (immigrant ethnic group) have opted for the treasury post and concede the Local Council chair to Basoga ethnic group, the perceived indigenous group in the region. Such arrangements, although they promote stability, are inimical to democratic processes and freedom of choice and cannot promote equality of opportunity'. We must add that democracy is a process and each local situation present unique problems that demand particular solutions. Our view is that this arrangement is better than a situation that breeds ethnic conflict and violence. There have been no violent ethnic conflicts in Bugiri district.

In practising the politics of expedience to keep political legitimacy in Kibaale, the President prevailed upon the chairman-elect to resign his post. The constitution clearly lays down procedures for the removal of a district chairperson. A chairperson can be removed by the council through a resolution supported by the votes of not less than two-thirds of all the members of the council, on the grounds of abuse of office, misconduct, physical incapacity or any other ground. If indeed the Movement's government interest was to democratise public life in the country, the chairman-elect would have been allowed to assume the office, and a process of his removal could have been initiated through council on any of the grounds mentioned.

Lastly, although the constitution provides for the President to take over a district administration, it explicitly states that this should be done with approval of two-thirds of all members of parliament in any of the following circumstances:

i) Where the district council so requests and it is in the public interest to do so;

ii) Where a state of emergency has been declared in that district or in Uganda generally;

iii) Where it has become extremely difficult or impossible for district government to function.

None of these circumstances prevailed in Kibaale. Although it had become impossible for Kibaale district to function because of the ethnic conflict, the President intervened without the approval of parliament. The President instead, by-passed parliament and convened a meeting of handpicked political actors who recommended the resignation of the chairman-elect. The chairman-elect was later promised a more high profile political job by the President.[19] This no doubt was a temporary solution, which could not solve the ethnic conflict. Above all the President's action undermined democratic governance in the country.

Conclusion

We have argued in this chapter that the Movement government has imitated, formulated and implemented policies and programmes to the extent that they give it political legitimacy. This tendency became more focused near, during and after elections. This to a great extent has led to negative developments in the polity such as ethnic conflict and violence. Ethnicity, as we pointed out, is a reality that cannot be wished away by legislation. We have argued elsewhere for example, that there is nothing wrong for a political party or any other organisation to have its initial power base or constituency within a particular ethnic group. What is important is for such political or other organisations that aspire for national objectives and ideals to evolve policies that embrace everybody regardless of ethnic identity. This cannot happen where a political party or any other organisation is limited in its political participation. We believe that South Africa had more complex land tenure systems under apartheid. But the commitment of African National Congress leadership to democracy saw a peaceful transition without giving birth to land-related ethnic conflict as in Kibaale district. This is not to suggest that the land question has been resolved in South Africa. The way forward therefore, is an enabling environment where individuals and groups can participate in the political process on their own terms, but within accepted rules. Can the Movement government ensure that environment?

Notes

1. The Banyoro who rejected the election of a Mukiga chairperson included important political and cultural leaders like the members of parliament from Bunyoro and Omukama (king) of Bunyoro kingdom, Solomon Gafabusa Iguru. See *The New Vision*, 21 and 25 March 2002, pp.1 and 2.
2. A. K. K. Mukwaya, 'Uganda's Movementocracy Experiment with Special Reference to the Great Lakes Region, 1986-2000', in T. Assefa (ed.) *Promoting Good Governance and Wider Civil Society Participation in Eastern and Southern Africa*, OSSREA, 2001, p. 64.
3. According to the 1995 Constitution, which has been referred to by some scholars as being an NRM document, this system can only be changed to any other, say a multiparty political system, through a referendum. After every period of five years, there must be referendum on a political system. Since its promulgation, a referendum has been held once in March 2001. The movement won by 70 percent. See The Uganda Electoral Commission Report for the March, 2001 Referendum.
4. K. Rupesinghe, 'Internal Conflicts and their Resolution: The Case of Uganda', in K. Rupesinghe (ed.) *Conflict Resolution in Uganda, Kampala*, James Currey, 1989, p. 3.
5. A. Syahuka-Muhindo, 'The Rwenzururu Movement and Democratic Struggle', in Mahmood Mamdani and Oloka-Onyango (eds.), *Uganda: Studies in Living Conditions, Popular Movements and Constitutionalism*, Kampala, Vienna, JEP Book Series, 1993, p. 276.
6. C. N. Chukwu, 'Ethnicity and Political Conflict in Nigeria', in P. G. Okoth and B.A. Ogot (eds), *Conflict in Contemporary Africa*, Nairobi, Kenya, Jomo Kenyatta Foundation, 2000, p. 141.
7. A. K. K. Mukwaya, *op cit*, p. 2.
8. See for example, M. Kulumba, 'Some Reflections on the Social-Political and Economic Reforms in Uganda Since 1986', Paper presented at the International Summer School of Cross-Cultural Studies, Under Polish Commission for UNESCO and Warsaw University Co-Sponsorship, Oriental Institute, University of Warsaw, August, 2001, p. 3.
9. A. B. Mujaju, 'Political Parties: What they are. How they arise and what they do', Inaugural Lecture delivered at Makerere University, 15 February 1996, p. 13.
10. J. Mugaju and J. Oloka-Onyango (eds.), *No Party Democracy in Uganda: Myths and Reality*, Kampala, Fountain Publishers, 2000, p. 5.

11. A. Juma Okuku, 'Ethnicity, State Power and the Democratization Process in Uganda', Paper presented at 'The Politics of African and Global Renewal: Challenges and Perspectives' conference, Durban, South Africa, 5-7 October 2001, p. 2.

12. In the May 2001 Presidential Elections for example, Y. Museveni was elected by the NRM executive Council l (NEC) to contest as a Movement presidential candidate.

13. Mailo land tenure is a form of land ownership introduced by the colonial state especially in Buganda. The tenure involves the holding of registered land in perpetuity while at the same time allowing the bona fide occupant to carry out developments on the land. See also A. Nuwagaba, 'The Political Economy of Land Management Regimes in Uganda: The Evolution of the Kibaale Question', Paper presented for Social Sector Planning and Management, Makerere University, 4 May 2002, p. 3.

14. The 'lost counties' historically included in addition to Buyaga and Bugangaizi, Rugojo (North Ssingo), Buruli and Buyaga (Bugerere). See S. R. Karugire, *A Political History of Uganda*, Nairobi, Heinemann Educational Books, 1987, p. 223.

15. S. R. Karugire (1987: 137).

16. For example Buganda demanded a federal arrangement during the Lancaster Independence Conference and in the 1995 Constitutional-Making debates during the Constituent Assembly. In the former she was granted a semi-federal arrangement, while in the latter, districts in Buganda were deemed to have cooperated after coming into force of the 1995 Constitution. See The 1962 Independence and The 1995 Constitutions.

17. *The New Vision*, 17 April 2002, p. 19.

18. Ebyaffe is a Luganda concept that embodies the Baganda's struggles to restore Buganda's kingdom including the assets that were confiscated in 1966 by the UPC government. The assets include among others the main palace at Mengo hill, Bulange (The seat of the kingdom government) and the 360 square miles of land in Buganda.

19. *The Monitor*, 20 April 2002, p. 1.

References

Bayart, J. F., 1993, *The State in Africa: The Politics of the Belly*, London and New York: Longman.

Chukwu, C. N., 2000, 'Ethnicity and Political Conflict in Nigeria', in P.G. Okoth and B.A. Ogot (eds.), *Conflict in Contemporary Africa*, Nairobi: Jomo Kenyatta Foundation.

Doornbos, M. and Mwesigye, F., 1997, 'The New Politics of Kingmaking', in H. R. Hansen and M. Twaddle (eds.), *From Chaos to Order: The Politics of Constitutional Making*, Kampala, London: Fountain Publishers.

Dunbar, A. R., 1965, *A History of Bunyoro-Kitara*, Nairobi: Oxford University Press.

Jorgensen, J. J., 1981, *Uganda: A Modern History*, London: Croom Helm Ltd.

Juma, Okuku, 2002, 'Ethnicity, State Power and Democratisation in Uganda', Discussion paper 17, Uppsala: Nordiska Afrikainstitutet.

Kabwegyere, T. B., 2000, *People's Choice, People's Power: Challenges and Prospects of Democracy in Uganda*, Kampala: Fountain Publishers.

Karugire, S. R., 1987, *A Political History of Uganda*, Nairobi, London: Heinemann Educational Books.

Kayunga S. S., 1995, 'Traditional Rulers and Decentralization in Africa: An Assessment', in P. Langseth et al (eds.), *Uganda: Landmarks in Rebuilding a Nation*, Kampala: Fountain Publishers.

Kiapi, A., 1989, 'The Constitution as a Mediator in Internal Conflict', in K. Rupesinghe (ed.), *Conflict Resolution in Uganda*, London, Athens: James Currey.

Kiwanuka, M. S. M., 1971, *A History of Buganda from the Foundation of the Kingdom to 1900*, London: Longman.

Kulumba, M., 2001, 'Some Reflections on the Social Political and Economic Reforms in Uganda Since 1986', Paper presented at the International Summer School of Cross-Cultural Studies, UNESCO and Warsaw Oriental Institute.

Low, A. D. and Pratt, R. C, eds., 1960, *Buganda and British Overrule*, London: New York, GUP.

Mamdani, Mahmood, 1976, *Politics & Class Formation in Uganda*, Nairobi, Ibadan, Lusaka, London: Heinemann.

Mamdani, Mahmood, 1996, *Citizen and Subject*, Kampala: Fountain Publishers.

Makara, M., Tukahebwa, G. B. & Byarugaba, E. F., eds., 1996, *Politics, Constitutionalism and Electioneering in Uganda: A Study of the 1994 Constituent Assembly Elections*, Kampala: Makerere University Press.

Makiika, M. R., 2002, 'Political Reforms in Uganda: Are the Traditional Institutions Marginalised?', Makerere Institute of Social Research Seminar Paper, Kampala, Makerere University.

Mugaju, J. and Oloka-Onyango J., eds., 2000, *No Party Democracy in Uganda: Myths and Reality*, Kampala: Fountain Publishers.

Mujaju, A. B., 1996, 'Political Parties: What They Are, How They Arise and What They Do', Inaugural professorial lecture, Makerere University.

Mukwaya, A. K. K., 2001, 'Uganda's Movementocracy Experiment with Special Reference to the Great Lakes Region, 1986–2000', in T. Assefa (ed.), *Promoting Good Governance and Wider Civil Society Participation*, Addis Ababa: OSSREA.

Nsibambi, A., 1989, 'The Land Question and Conflict', in R. Kumar (ed.), *Conflict Resolution in Uganda*, London, Athens: James Currey.

Nsibambi, A. R., 1997, 'The Restoration of Traditional Rulers', in H. B. Hansen and M. Twaddle (eds.), *From Chaos to Order: The Politics of Constitutional Making in Uganda*, Kampala: Fountain Publishers.

Nuwagaba, A., 2002, 'The Political Economy of Land Management Regimes in Uganda: The Evolution of Kibaale Question', Paper presented for Social Sector Planning and Management, Makerere University.

Oloka-Onyango, J., 2000, 'New Wine or New Bottles? Movement Politics and One-Partyism in Uganda', in J. Mugaju & J. Oloka-Onyango (eds.), *No Party Democracy in Uganda: Myths and Realities*, Kampala: Fountain Publishers.

Parekh, M., 1993, 'From Resistance Movement to One-Party State', Department of Political Science & Public Administration, Seminar Paper, Kampala, Makerere University.

Richards, A. I., 1960, *A Study of Political Development in Some Uganda and Tanganyika Tribes*, London: Faber and Faber.

Roberts, A. D., 1962, 'The Lost Counties of Bunyoro', in Gertzel et al (eds.), *The Uganda Journal*, 26, (2).

Rupesinghe, Kumar, ed., 1989, *Conflict Resolution in Uganda*, London, Athens: James Currey.

Syahuka-Muhindo, 1993, 'The Rwenzuru Movement and Democratic Struggle', in Mahmood Mamdani and J. Oloka-Onyango (eds.), *Uganda: Studies in Living Conditions, Popular Movements and Constitutionalism*, Kampala, Vienna: JEP Book Series.

The *1992 Constitution of Uganda*.

The *1995 Republican Constitution of Uganda*.

The *1998 Land Act*.

The *March 2001 Referendum Report*, The *Uganda Electoral Commission Series*.

8

Transient, Mobile 'Nations' and the Dilemma of Nationhood in the Horn of Africa: Interrogating Nomadic Pastoralists, Insecurity and the Uncertainty of Belonging

Maurice N. Amutabi

Introduction

The Horn of Africa is home to the largest concentration of pastoralists in the world. It has also witnessed perhaps the largest number of nationalist uprisings in Africa. In this chapter, I scrutinise the absence of physical and emotional belonging and attachment that is often displayed by pastoralist peoples through their actions, often seen as unpatriotic, such as raiding, banditry, rustling and the killing of fellow countrymen for cattle. I assess the place of transient and migratory ethnic groups in the nation-state, especially their lack of fixed abodes in any one country, and how this plays out in the countries of the region. I pay special attention to cross-border migratory ethnic groups that inhabit the semi-desert areas of the Sudan-Kenya-Ethiopia-Somalia borderlines as case studies. The paper will focus on the Shangilla and Oromo (Borana) of Kenya and Ethiopia, Turkana of Kenya, Nyangatom (Merile), Dongiro, Dassanetch and Anyuak of Ethiopia, Toposa of Sudan and Uganda and the Jie and Karimojong of Uganda.

It is my contention that this volatile security 'fault line' consisting of 'transient nations' has not received the required scholarly attention. Issues of patriotism, nationalism and nationhood have never been thoroughly interrogated vis-à-vis these nomadic pastoralists. To which countries do these migratory groups belong? Can they be incorporated? I argue that the lack of nomadic pastoralist heroes and heroines, the marginalisation of their traditions and cultures, are to blame for their indifference and ambivalence. Further, I argue that lack of proper policies and appreciation of these 'transient' or 'mobile', or even 'seasonal', nations by governments of the region are to blame for their continued existence outside the realm of nationhood. I point out that the seasonal migratory pattern of ethnic groups such as the Shangilla who live half a year in Kenya and the other half in Ethiopia according to the incidence of rain, opens up more gaps of alienation and further distance from nation-state ideals. The common denominator in this transient or mobile character of pastoralists is livestock.

Livestock are at the centre of my assessment of these transient nations. In fact, livestock are always at the centre of migratory and transient ethnic groups of the Horn. The political economy of livestock, which are treasured resources, the source of life and wealth, and also, the cause of wars and conflicts among the pastoralist peoples of the Horn of Africa, therefore constitute a very significant component of this paper. The contention of this paper is that to understand the characteristics and nature of pastoralist ethnic groups of the Horn, one has to examine livestock as both a commodity and a cultural artefact, with its attendant attributes. Among pastoralists, livestock represent life. They are pivotal to the wars, conflicts and bandit activities in the region. By and large, the combatants search, raid and kill for livestock. Livestock comprise the mainstay of livelihoods in this region. I point out that the Horn of Africa and its environs is just an arena, a theatre of sorts, in which greater global issues and rivalries have been and continue to be played out, and that the 'beasts of war' (livestock) are mere catalysts and pawns.

The Horn of Africa, which is a recipient of spill over effects from armed conflicts in Somalia, Southern Ethiopia, Northern Kenya, Southern Sudan and Northern Uganda, is a death trap; a security nightmare for all governing authorities surrounding it, legitimate or illegitimate. The actors pursue personal, clan, ethnic and national objectives. Thus all the combatants in these conflicts are dug in and determined to pursue their objectives to the end however illogical they may seem. Livestock as reported in all raids and skirmishes, is the main denominator to all the combatants and is likely to remain so until peace or alternative economic avenues and ways of livelihood come to the Horn of Africa and its environs.

The problems afflicting this part of Eastern Africa have their origins in globalisation due to the fact that all the combatants have a certain connection to global forces in history. It is my contention that the Somali state broke up after Siad Barre's regime was brought down in a rebel onslaught that was a direct impact of the collapse of the Soviet Union; that the Sudan People's Liberation Movement receives support from the international community on the ideological pretext of fighting Islamic fundamentalism associated with the Khartoum government; that the pastoralist ethnic groups in the Horn of Africa because of the availability of AK-47 assault rifles which they obtain easily through wars in the region are connected with global forces; that the Lord's Resistance Army as financed by the Khartoum government is a counter measure against Uganda's support of the SPLM/A and therefore the other external forces. The cellular phones, the powerful radio communications equipment used today by cattle raiders and soldiers, the modern war machines and weapons, are all factors of globalisation. Thus, by and large, in as much as the problems of the Horn of Africa may be about livestock, they are also about international ideological scheming and counter-scheming. Select examples of a few of the ethnic groups in the region are highlighted to address the relationship between livestock and bandit activities in the Horn of Africa in particular and the region in general.

Globalisation and Militarisation in the Horn of Africa

The Horn of Africa has a very long and prominent standing in the global historiography of Eastern Africa. The strands of globalisation in the Horn go back many centuries ago to the period of colonial advent. Modern militarisation and the rush for arms in the Horn of Africa in particular, and Eastern Africa as a whole started in 1914 during World War One when combatants were recruited from the region and participated in warfare. This build-up of small arms and light weapons was exacerbated in 1937 when the Italians occupied the Lower Omo Valley and incorporated the local people (the Merile and Nyangatom) in their army, and rallied them against the British. One thousand rifles were distributed among these people in order to help the Italians to stop or prevent Ethiopian and British counter attacks. Armed with these superior weapons, the Nyangatom and Merile raided the Turkana in 1937. In this attack, the Turkana lost 300 men. The British, with a column of the King's African Rifles, retaliated on behalf of the Turkana who were now subjects of the British Empire and killed 24 Merile and seized some livestock (Tornay 1993:159). The arming of the local pastoralists against their neighbours intensified when the British recruited 5,000 Turkana in their offensive against the Italians, Merile (Dassanetch) and Nyangatom (Dongiro) between 1940 and 1941. The British forces were victorious, and by extension the Turkana also, and occupied the Lower Omo Valley which today lies in Ethiopia, driving away the Italian forces. The Somali were also recruited mainly from Kismayu and used by the British in their expeditions of pacification against many pastoralist groups in the region between 1914 and 1936 (Aguilar 1998:260-61; Nangulu 2000:23).

Livestock constitute the lifeline of the people in the Horn of Africa. The Horn of Africa has witnessed internecine ethnic conflicts emanating from scarcity of resources and, as Lamphear has noted, the 'desire to capture livestock, to gain access to natural resources (Lamphear 1994:69). Most often, pastoralists fight among themselves. The fighting is usually to establish rights over pastureland and water where sharing rights have broken down due to misunderstandings or scarcity. But such sharing of pasture, water and even livestock is often negotiated. There are well-defined traditional systems of utilisation of the grazing areas through established migration routes, and leading to the conservation of grass and watering points. When there is no alternative to negotiation, especially when friendly neighbours have all lost herds, raiding becomes the only viable alternative for replenishing stock and for survival. Traditionally, raiding was a cultural enterprise carried out strictly for restocking purposes among pastoralists. Raiding was used to replenish depleted herds. After drought or when disease ravaged herds of one group, pastoralists often negotiated for seed stock among their neighbours which they paid back after replenishment and stability. As such, raiding was a last resort when the loan system had failed or when the whole neighbourhood where such seed animals could be borrowed were equally in short supply. Cattle lending is an ancient practice among pastoralists where one clan provided seed animals to a neighbouring one for restocking. After herds recovered, an equal number of seed animals were usually returned to the lender. This was carried out between friendly pastoralist groups. Raiding was a last resort when such schemes had failed.

There was a great deal of reciprocity in raiding where groups came together to help each other in restocking through voluntary exchange or raiding (Muller 1989). Women and children were never killed during raids and calves were never taken. Where captives were taken, assimilation not annihilation of rival communities was usually the rule (Lamphear 1994:69). Raiding was thus relatively humane. As such, raiding was carried out under the command of elders who ensured that ethics were adhered to. Elders acted usually in opposition to the young men's aggressive tendencies, which might have led to the unwelcome expansion of conflict and undercut the authority and pre-eminence of the older men. 'War', Paul Baxter (1979) has remarked, 'was too serious a matter to be left to the young'. The generation system, therefore, provided an important means by which elders could exert authority over truculent juniors and impose strict limitations on warfare itself (Almogor 1979; Baxter 1979; Galaty 1987).

From his many years of study of pastoralists, Lamphear avers that 'Most military activity took the form of intermittent raiding rather than anything like large-scale campaigns and typically, it stemmed from a desire to capture livestock, to gain access to natural resources' (Lamphear 1994:69). Escalation of violence in the region and increasing toll on human life in raids indicates the breakdown of the traditional system of sanctity of human life and reciprocity in raiding among pastoralists. The new form of raiding is sometimes carried out for such obscure reasons as mere military reputation and prestige (Dent 1977; Parker 1988). A new hierarchy based on the potential and capacity to amass tools of violence, especially modern arms, in essence, creation of warlords and bandits, has replaced elders leading, to escalation of armed conflict (Amutabi 1995, 1999).

More recently, the problems in the Ethiopian State, especially the Ogaden war between Ethiopia and Somalia and wars of liberation of the Eritreans, Tigreans and Oromo, have led to the amassing of arms. In the Sudan, the Sudanese government has had intermittent clashes with Southern rebels since the Anya nya movement in 1952, and which was revived more earnestly with the SPLA activities from 1983. They not only made available arms in exchange for livestock, but also provided a market for the raided stock for rebel camps. The clan struggle for state power in Somalia in the 1990s has also led to flow of arms in the Triangle. In Uganda, the Lord's Resistance Army has impacted on the pastoralist lives in the entire northern rim of the country. This area is near the Triangle, and its location facilitates the infiltration of arms and the supply of livestock for meat in the military camps (Amutabi 1999).

Militarisation has led to the acquisition of weapons by different ethnic groups for survival. The more sophisticated arms a group acquired compared to others in the region, the more dominant it became. Thus the dominance of certain pastoralist groups in the region measured by size of herds and the creation of grazing areas and access to watering points, bears a direct correlation to the availability of sophisticated arms. The arms rush, which started in the Horn of Africa, has thus led to spill over effects spreading to the whole region. Today, this area occupied by the Turkana, Gabra, Boran, Burji, Pokot, Rendille, El Molo, Shangilla, Oromo, Merile (Dassanetch), Mursi, Nyangatom (Dongiro), Bodi, Arsi, Toposa, Karimojong, Jie, Afar, the Somalia clan families of Degodia, Hawiye, Aulihyan, Darod, Mohammed Zuber (MD), Abduwak, Gashes, Ogaden, Issa, among others, is awash with automatic and sophisticated military gear that would be the envy of many modern armies of some countries in Africa. Kenya, Ethiopia, Sudan, Uganda and Somalia have experienced the effects of the Triangle. This is one of the most volatile areas in Africa and has the greatest concentration of arms from the heaviest to the lightest.

Conflict among pastoralists in Eastern Africa recently has taken on new exaggerated dimensions. A shrinking resource base has provoked desperate struggles for survival, in which the very existence of these groups is threatened. Raiding and counter raiding for livestock has given way to commercial raiding. This last phenomenon has been brought about by the great demand for meat by the various combatants in the area. The combatants have included those from Somalia where there is internecine warring between various factions; in Southern Ethiopia, the Oromo Liberation (OLF) front is engaged in a war of attrition with the Addis Ababa government; in Northern Kenya, the Pokot livestock raiders are continuing their plunder and massacre in Turkana, Marakwet, Samburu and Rendille, where Kenya's security personnel have lost the initiative; in Southern Sudan, the Sudan People's Liberation Movement/Army (SPLM/A) has believed since 1983 that it is on the verge of founding a new state; in Northern Uganda, the Lord's Resistance Army has remained an intransigent enigma to Yoweri Museveni's government. Having depleted the area of its wild animals, livestock is the only resource readily available to the combatants and their neighbours who have been forced to build up their military arsenal to survive. These are the issues that this paper addresses.

Why Pastoralists Are Transient and Mobile in the Horn of Africa

The Horn of Africa 'is home to the largest remaining aggregation of traditional livestock producers in the world' (Markakis 1998:41). I will use the Ilemi Triangle and its fringe to demonstrate some of the problems in this entire region. The Triangle is the area between Ethiopia, Kenya, Sudan and Uganda. Most of these pastoralist economies which are found in incredibly rugged terrain, punishing climate and extreme temperatures, vegetation covered with shrubs and needle-sharp thorns, with snakes, centipedes, scorpions and other wild creatures and animals, are interconnected in ways that make nonsense of the so-called international border demarcations. As a consequence, the pastoralist regions are less policed and their border areas more porous than other border points in the region. There is hardly any major pastoral group that lives entirely within the boundaries of one state in Eastern Africa. Even where this is not the case, the group would have closely related groups across the border. Pastoralists in the border areas like the Turkana, Toposa, Merile, Karimojong, and Boran have established alliances with their cousins across the border. In some cases like among the Oromo of Ethiopia and Somali of Kenya, they have joined the liberation movements seeking separation or greater autonomy from the centralised states of Eastern Africa. In other cases, the individual groups have asserted their superiority over neighbours by the use of arms through internecine raids. Despite this conflict, there are continuous flows of people, arms and livestock across the borders through raids and smuggling, which has escalated raiding and degeneration into bandit activities. These raids for livestock and subsequent counter raids and banditry can be attributed to several factors.

First, the pastoralists have no regard for international boundaries and consider them non-existent. They depend for their livelihood on an environment dictated by climatic conditions under whose mercy they operate, where seasonal movements through known migratory routes, patterns of pasture availability and water sources, established kinship networks, and long standing traditional cultural and political alliances, provide the bases for their way of existence. The resources upon which pastoralists depend for their livelihood are spread sometimes beyond national boundaries. The state supervision of territorial boundaries interferes with the survival of pastoralists based on seasonal movement in search of pasture and water. This is the underlying reason why ethnic groups in the Horn of Africa have very little or no notion of boundaries.

In this regard, the Shangilla do not have a permanent abode and move with their livestock between Kenya and Ethiopia in order to utilise their traditional seasonal grazing and watering points. This movement is one of the ways through which arms infiltrate across borders. On one of our visits to this area in Kenya, we found them on the Ethiopian side. During another visit, they had come back as a result of improved pasture due to rain. Those that I interviewed were noncommittal about their nationality and preferred to leave the issue of citizenship as vague as possible. The Boran of Kenya are allied to the Oromo of Ethiopia under the Gada system which is a traditional structure linking Oromia speakers throughout the world. They thus cross the borders frequently in meeting the demands and exigencies of the Gada (Aguilar 1998:257; Fugich 1999:5).

The Nyangatom of the Lower Omo Valley are another example of a people whose traditional territory has been cut in two by an international boundary. The Nyakua River that has marked the border between Ethiopia and the Sudan since 1908, is in fact the centre of the Nyangatom pastoral ecosystem, with Nyangatom (Dongiro) in Ethiopia and their Nyangatom cousins the Toposa in Sudan. Tornay notes that 'since long before the Ethiopian troops of Menelek annexed the area of the Lower Omo Valley at the turn of the century, the Nyangatom have been migrating with their herds to and from the western marches, thus maintaining close contact' with their Sudanese cousins, the Toposa' (Tornay 1993:155). The Anyuak found on both sides of the Ethiopian and Sudanese borders constitute another example of an ethnicity divided by arbitrary colonial boundaries in Eastern Africa (Perner 1993:125).

Second, pastoralists live exclusively off the herd and its products. The recurrence of drought and famine in their terrain and various epidemics has made pastoralists increasingly dependent on the import of grain from other regions – besides raiding. Their consumption patterns have changed, and in the recent past have been captured by global tastes as they have become dependent on local and international markets to sell their livestock and livestock products in order to purchase grain and manufactured goods. The exchanges have gone beyond their traditional markets made up mainly by the cultivators on their fringes with whom they traded. Nowadays, pastoralists on the border usually extend their domain of trade to markets and urban centres across state boundaries where they obtain their supply of modern products. Some groups consider such markets a natural extension of their traditional territory and part of wider social and economic networks essential for their survival.

Unfortunately, such markets, towns and surrounding areas have often been incorporated into the pastoralist realm and subjected to cross-border raids for food, livestock and arms. This is the fate that has befallen many towns in the pastoralist fringe, which have experienced sporadic pastoralist raids. Such towns include Kaabong and Loyoro in Uganda; Lokichokio, Kibish, Todentang, Sololo, Banisa, Malka Mari, Moyale and Rhamu in Kenya; Kelem, Mega, Chelago, Maji, and Moyale in Ethiopia; and Lutuke, Nagpotpot, Kapoeta, Loeli and Nagichot in Sudan. Small arms and other military gear are sold in many of these towns in underground markets and the pastoralists are known to be the avenues for the cross-border trading and channelling of these weapons. Many respondents, on condition of anonymity, admitted that such information on arms transfer and even the whereabouts of markets were common and also known to security personnel of the respective countries. It appears that the security personnel have reluctantly accepted the position, the argument perhaps being that for a group to repulse raids from other ethnic groups in this region, the appropriate weapons are required. There were many cases where we spotted herd-boys armed with AK-47s and other assault machine guns, especially among the Turkana (Amutabi 1999). At times, these arms in youthful hands are often put to reckless use for self-aggrandisement and even amusement in what is increasingly turning into bandit activities rather than raiding for livestock.

Raiding for livestock across ethnic and national borders among the pastoralists in Eastern Africa is legion (Amutabi 1999; Turton 1977, 1988, 1989, 1994; Fukui 1994; Lamphear 1994; Allen 1994; Baxter 1994 and Tornay 1993). These studies indicate the centrality of herds and related resources in the pastoralist economies and their survival. Tornay illustrates the point when he shows how the Nyangatom (Dongiro) have been more or less continuously at war with almost all their neighbours throughout their history. In an impressive chronology of raids and counter raids by the Nyangatom (Dongiro) with their neighbours such as the Merile (Dassanetch), the Mursi, the Kara, the Bodo and the Turkana, Tornay illustrates the impact of livestock raiding in the military balance of the region (Tornay 1993:143-163).

Third, the creation of national parks, game reserves and other wildlife conservation sanctuaries and schemes within the pastoralist ranges by governments, has meant reduced grazing space and has reduced the supply of game meat supplement to pastoralist groups. There are several parks and game sanctuaries within a distance of 500 square kilometres of the Ilemi Triangle in particular, and the Horn of Africa in general. These include the Omo National Park, Tama Wildlife Reserve, Mago National Park and Stephanie Wildlife Reserve in Ethiopia, Siboloi National Park in Kenya and Kidepo National Park in Uganda. There have often been armed and violent confrontations between pastoralists and park guards, game rangers and security personnel over park animals, especially during dry seasons when livestock numbers are down (Amutabi 1999; Gufu 1998). Less pasture has meant fewer and poorer quality livestock herds. Prevention of hunting in the gazetted and protected game sanctuaries has meant that the traditional supplements of game meat have been eliminated. The whole pressure has therefore been transferred to the existing livestock and the pressure has escalated cross-border raiding. To many pastoralists, it is easier to face fellow pastoralist groups in armed confrontation over livestock, than engaging security personnel over wildlife meat. This has meant more raids for livestock than hunting for wildlife.

Fourth, the plight of the pastoralist has been exacerbated by the introduction of cultivation in the arid and semi-arid lands through irrigation. This process, mainly fronted by foreign donor agencies and Non-Governmental Organizations (NGOs) keen on removing the dependency of pastoralists on aid and on the vulnerable livestock sector, has deprived pastoralists of valuable pasture. Permanent water sources have also been reduced through the diversion of water into irrigation canals. Many seasonal rivers that are now increasingly used in irrigation schemes are rendered dry most of the year, and this has led to the death of livestock, occasioning more pressure on the few herds in the area. The result has been more raids and counter raids where livestock remain the common denominator. Tornay describes such a scheme in Kibish at Kangaten by World Vision, an international NGO, which allowed the cultivation of some 25 hectares of sorghum by Nyangatom, Kara and Mursi, and explains its incompatibility among these pastoralist peoples (Tornay 1993:147).

Fifth, the reduction of pastoralist mobility has increasingly been restricted within each state by provincial, district and local boundaries for disease control and quarantine. This has limited the circulation of livestock in the pastoralist range, causing imbalances in the region. This also causes ecological disequilibrium (Coppock 1994; Behnke 1993; Helland 1993; Scoones 1995; Gufu 1998). Too great a build-up of herds in one area attracts the attention of raiders from other places where scarcity prevails. This has been the fate of the Turkana of Kenya, for example, in the 1990s. Due to the improvement in veterinary services sponsored by foreign NGOs like the CARE International, OXFAM, Heifer International, among others, the Turkana have in the past ten years built up impressive stocks. Within this period, the Turkana lost the highest number of lives in a single year in their recorded history. For example on a single day, on 6th September1997 in Lokitang, the Turkana suffered one of the worst raids in their territory in the hands of their Merile neighbours. In that raid, they lost over 7000 goats and sheep, 400 camels and 42 people were killed (Amutabi 1999:4; *Daily Nation*, September 7, 1997:12).

Sixth, arms acquisitions in the region and the demand for livestock in military camps in the Oromo Liberation Movement (OLF) occupied areas in Ethiopia; in the Southern People's Liberation Army (SPLA) camps in Sudan; in various warlord camps in Somalia; and in the Lord's Resistance Army (LRA) camps in Uganda among others, have all exacerbated raiding for livestock in the region. The market dynamics have been altered by these new and increased demands. Livestock prices have thus risen from the 1990s because the livestock were exchanged for arms or for money. Tornay reports that 'some Kibish people went to Sudan to exchange cattle for automatic weapons. They say that in this way, they acquired several hundreds of these weapons and that they are now better armed than they have ever been...' (Tornay 1993:148). Having superior arms meant easy access to livestock. This in turn promoted a lack of incentive to build livestock numbers. Instead, pastoralist groups focussed on acquiring arms and the creation of raiding parties as the easy way out.

On availability of arms, Markakis asserts that 'in a region awash with automatic weapons, and large groups of heavily armed men waging political struggles from bases in the bush, conditions are not normal. Under these conditions, animals are likely to disappear completely from the vicinity' (Markakis 1998:46). Tornay reports that in 1991, 'twenty five young Nyangatom (Merile) had been trained in an EPRDF (Ethiopia People's Republic Democratic Front) camp in Awasa and they had been sent back to their country with Kalashnikovs, as purely tribal militia, committed to maintain local order under the guidance of their elders' (Tornay 1993:151). He reports also that 'the Sudanese Toposa have made an alliance with the Sudan People's Liberation Army (SPLA), from which they acquired automatic weapons' (Tornay 1993:148). It is not surprising that from the Somalia-Ethiopia-Kenya border area in the east, to the Sudan-Kenya-Ethiopia border area in the west, one notices an increasing number of families that have completely been de-stocked through raids and reduced to destitution. These families have fled their homelands and moved across borders, like Ethiopians, Sudanese and Somali refugees in Kenya, and Kenyan refugees in Ethiopia. Other de-stocked pastoralists have resigned themselves to becoming internal refugees in camps around churches or crowded into peri-urban slums in the region. Commenting on this arms build-up in the area, Perner has stated: 'The fact that insurgent groups have through the years of struggle and war acquired a great amount of sophisticated weapons, is of great concern in this respect' (Perner 1993:133).

At the United Nations High Commission for Refugees (UNHCR) camp at Kakuma, there are very many de-stocked destitute Turkana families outside the camp, numbering almost half of the refugees inside the camp. These Turkana families depend on handouts for survival, as relief has become their main source of sustenance. Occasionally, they are able to carry out menial tasks around and inside the camp for little pay. The same holds with regard to Dadaab and Hagdera UNHCR refugee camps in northeastern, where there are many Kenyan internal refugees besides Somalians and Ethiopians. Owino Opondo reported in the *Daily Nation* of 21 January 2001 that more than 600 Burji, Gabra and Boran families had fled their Moyale constituency homes following invasions from the Ethiopian side of the border. Many ended up in Walda Refugee camp that has been building up in refugee numbers from Kenya, Ethiopia and Somalia. On escalation of bandit attacks, the Moyale Member of Parliament is quoted in Opondo's report above as saying that 'Six villages in my constituency are now desolate as residents have fled their homes and are camping at the Moyale divisional headquarters (Opondo 2001). The affected villages were Kiltipe, Uran, Lataka, Uran Dida, Badanota and Kicha that are on the Kenyan side of the border with Ethiopia. Thus, the economies of the pastoralist groups in the region have been destroyed and their homelands depopulated.

Seventh, improved marketing for livestock and their products in the region and in external markets has led to greater demand. As a result, buying cartels have developed, and very aggressive middlemen are involved in livestock marketing. Because of the scarcity of livestock in traditional areas due to raiding, these cartels and middlemen organise and sponsor their own raids by hiring mercenaries and bandits. Thus traditional raiding customs and 'etiquette' where children and women were spared and male causalities limited, have been eliminated and replaced with merciless raiding practices by private armies where a whole family or clan can be completely wiped out in a single raid. The armies engage in bandit activities when not raiding for livestock, and the result has been escalation of insecurity in the region. Reports of attacks carried out with uncanny military precision are legion.

In June 1971, Merile (Dassanetch) herdsmen massacred at least 200 Dongiro (Nyangatom) from several Kibish settlements in a single attack (Tornay 1993:144). Turton visited the Mursi in December 1987 and reported that the Nyangatom had massacred a large Mursi settlement on 21 February 1987 (Turton 1993). The report by Tornay of an attack by the Nyangatom on a Kenyan police station at Kibish demonstrates how bold these groups have become. Such attacks on police stations and military installations have become more common in the region in the recent past (Amutabi 1999).

In July 1999, a daredevil military raid occurred simultaneously in Moyale town on the Kenyan and Ethiopian side where property of unknown value was stolen. The Ethiopian government blamed the attack on the rebel Oromo Liberation Front (OLF) militia, but the Kenyan authorities laid the blame on Ethiopian security personnel. In January, Ethiopian bandits attacked and abducted a Kenyan policeman after ambushing a Government security team at Kiltipe. Eight Kenya police officers and two residents were killed in the attack. The abducted policeman was allegedly being held at Bokuluboma, about 140 kilometres inside Ethiopia (Opondo 2001). The OLF's militia has fought the Addis Ababa regime for more than five years. The Ethiopian government has been accusing Nairobi of hosting the OLF, whose troops it pursues deep into the Kenyan side, leaving a trail of deaths and loss of property.

On 7 July 2001, the *Daily Nation* reported that five people had been killed in a week-long outbreak of violence between Turkana of Kenya and Toposa of Sudan on their common border. Two Catholic nuns were also raped and livestock stolen. It was reported that the raiding had started on the previous week when Turkana raiders killed a Toposa youth on the Sudanese side. The Toposa hit back at Turkana pastoralists in Lokichokio town and stole more than 400 head of cattle. The report said that 'two of the raiders, described as notorious criminals, were killed in the attack and three guns recovered by Turkana herdsmen (*Daily Nation*, 7 July 2001). The report goes further and says that 'Toposa bandits later attacked three vehicles travelling to Lokichokio town, looted luggage and raped two Catholic nuns travelling in one of the vehicles belonging to the Diocese of Torit' (ibid.). This story confirms that raiding is no longer carried out under the traditional auspices of replenishing of pastoralist stock, but for purely malicious and selfish, even satanic motives like rape and looting of non-pastoralist items and resources.

On 11 May 2001, the *Daily Nation* carried a feature article on what it termed 'Kenya's Kosovo', which is a stretch of land in a place known as Baragoi next to the Kenya-Ethiopia-Sudan border on the fringe of the Ilemi Triangle. Because of the prevalence of dangerous arms previously used in livestock raids and counter raids and now used on ethnic altercations, the area has been called Kenya's Kosovo, which is reminiscent of Kosovo, the war-torn area in the Balkan. The story pointed out that because of banditry, Baragoi, which lies in a purely pastoralist zone, was one of the most dangerous places in Kenya. Baragoi is just a few kilometres from Suguta Valley, a security nightmare to security personnel in Kenya and a haven of livestock thieves and bandits from Kenya, Ethiopia and Sudan. Because of this valley's treacherous terrain and unbearable temperatures, heat index and humidity, Kenyan security personnel and even local people like the Samburu fear it and all readily admit so. 'Even children know this. They welcome visitors chanting: "Welcome to Kosovo! Baragoi is Kosovo!"' (Agutu and Kariuki 2001). In 1996 a helicopter carrying senior Kenya government officials together with the then Samburu District Commissioner James Nyandoro on a security mission was blown to smithereens by bandits in Suguta Valley (Amutabi 1999).

Agutu and Kariuki assert that 'for five years now, Baragoi residents have suffered all manner of war; from bandit attacks to cattle rustling to thuggery. All the aggressors wield AK-47 assault rifles and other arms, ever ready to fire' (Agutu and Kariuki 2001). The government of Kenya has responded by deploying a battery of military equipment and personnel into the area yet the killings continue unabated. The area has become a military operation zone, where 'groups of people travelling along the Baragoi-Maralal route must have armed escort. Barely a week passes without a convoy being attacked by bandits hiding in the harsh terrain of the 200km stretch. In the beginning, it was mere cattle rustling and rarely would raiders kill. Then banditry followed. Neither young nor old, resident nor visitor, women nor children, are spared. And now robbers have set camp, looting homes and shops without a care in the world' (Agutu and Kariuki 2001).

Concluding Remarks

From the foregoing discussion, certain recommendations and concluding remarks can be made. Due to the escalation of violence in the Horn of Africa and its environs, some pastoralist communities are threatened with imminent extinction in this anarchistic survival of the fittest. The ethnic centres of most of the pastoralist groups in Eastern Africa have shifted in the past twenty years due to raids and fear of counter raids. Since these groups fallaciously believe that the panacea for their survival is the acquisition of yet more sophisticated arms, they are building death traps in which they might all ultimately perish. Fear and uncertainly now reign in the region. One encounters wide unutilised corridors between these groups, which would be better harnessed for grazing purposes.

Groups are finding themselves occupying less space as they push away from areas of contact. The area between Kenya's Turkana and Uganda's Karimojong is a virtual empty space. The same is the case with regard to the border area between the Turkana and the Toposa of Sudan and the Turkana and the Dongiro, and the Merile of Ethiopia on their common borders. There is a chain reaction sequence that results from this shifting of spaces. In Ethiopia, as the Nyangatom and the Dassanetch who neighbour the Kenyan Turkana push themselves northwards, they in turn push away their northern neighbours like the Kara, Beshada, Hamar, Koegu, Kwegu, Mursi, and the Bodi. The Turkana have also caused the Samburu, Rendille, El Molo and Pokot to move and adjust their ethnic space within Kenya. Similarly the Karimojong push inside Uganda as a result of withdrawal from border areas has impacted on the space of the Jie, the Labwor and the Dodos.

Stock theft, raiding, rustling or banditry and killing of humans have escalated to very dangerous levels not just in the Ilemi Triangle, but also in Eastern Africa as a whole. The security of the region is in great danger of getting out of hand, as not all the governments in the region are fully committed to the eradication of conflict in the area. Some of the governments are not to blame because they do not have full control of pastoralist areas, as in the case of the Sudan. The Inter-Governmental Authority on Development (IGAD) has not been able to come up with a working formula for forestalling armed conflict in the area. The governments in the region must spend more funds in arming their security personnel beyond the traditional G.3 rifles if they expect their presence to be felt in this very militarised zone, and to be able to operate joint policing of the region. Air power, especially helicopters, and other superior combat gear should be considered. Any government must have monopoly of force if it has to succeed in restoring control of an area such as the Horn of Africa.

Military garrisons and police posts should be increased in the areas adjacent to the Horn of Africa; in Somalia, Uganda, Ethiopia, the New Sudan and Kenya. The use of armed village vigilante groups should also be encouraged, as they will deter raiding by bands who sneak behind government security forces. Pastoralists should be made to understand that it is they who will determine their own fate. Later on, each government should be entrusted to disarm their pastoralists when they eventually attain full control of them. Armed conflict among the Karimojong went down when all Karimojong adults were trained and armed in the highly successful 'chaka mchaka' (village vigilante) programme. The only danger has been that when the same Ugandan government wanted to disarm them for attacking unarmed groups, the Karimojong repulsed government forces. Karimojong possess over one million guns; more than the less than half-million government soldiers.

The existing governments in the region should also introduce sophisticated methods of branding, labelling or tagging and identification of animals.

Microcomputer chips with an electronic code number for each animal, as is currently the practice in Denmark, New Zealand and Australia and in South Africa, to track down herds should be implanted in pastoralist animals through incisions on ears, necks and the like. This will help in tracking down stolen animals even across national borders. This will help in making identification of stolen animals easy, and stock theft will become a futile endeavour. Perennial raiders like Nyangatom, Toposa, Karimojong, Jie, Turkana and Pokot will settle down to producing their own animals instead of their current reliance on stock theft. In this case, veterinary officers who have been rendered jobless in the region should be used to check the identity of every animal slaughtered or exported by verifying information from the microchips.

The NGOs should be given more leeway in bringing about peace through mediation, conflict resolution and poverty reduction strategies. NGOs and Community Based Organisations (CBOs) operate among these groups on everyday basis and even have ways of knowing the belligerent and recalcitrant elements. Raiding escalates in periods of acute scarcity. Thus poverty eradication programmes like restocking, drilling of bore-holes, building of dams and rain water harvest projects, improvement of roads in pastoralist regions, close policing, establishment of village banks, among others, should be used to reduce conflict. The governments have parceled out traditional pastoralist grazing areas and hunting grounds and converted them into wildlife sanctuaries, which earn them a lot of income from tourism. They should plough back these incomes into pastoralist areas.

Acknowledgement

I would like to acknowledge the contribution of the Social Science Research Council (SSRC), Action-Aid (Kenya), Association for World Education (AWE-Kenya) which sponsored various research activities on which this paper is based.

References

Aguilar, I.M., 1998, 'Reinventing Gada: Generational Knowledge in Boorana', in M.Aguilar (ed,), *The Politics of Age and Gerontocracy in Africa: Ethnographies of the Past and Memories of the Present*, Trenton, New Jersey and Asmara, Eritrea: Africa World Press, pp. 257-279.

Agutu, M and Kariuki, J., 2001, 'Welcome to Kenya's Kosovo', *Daily Nation*, May 11, 2001.

Allen, T., 1994, 'Ethnicity and Tribalism on the Sudan-Uganda Border', in K. Fukui and J. Markakis, (eds.), *Ethnicity and Conflict in the Horn of Africa*, London and Athens: James Currey and Ohio University Press, pp.112-139.

Almagor, U., 1979, 'Raiders and Elders: A Confrontation of Generations Among the Dassanetch', in K. Fukui and D. Turton, (eds.), *Warfare among East African*

Herders, Osaka: Senri Ethnological Foundation, National Museum of Ethnology.

Alverson, J. A., 1989, *Starvation and Peace or Food and War? Aspects of Armed Conflicts in the Lower Omo Valley*, Ethiopia, Uppsala, Research Reports in Cultural Anthropology.

Amutabi, M. N., 1999, 'Cattle Rustling Among Pastoralists in Northern Kenya: The Genesis and the Truth', Paper presented at conference on Community Education co-hosted by Action-Aid and Association for World Education (AWE), Isiolo, Kenya, August 25th-28th, 1999.

Amutabi, M. N., 1995, 'Challenging the Orthodoxies: The Role of Ethnicity and Regional Nationalism in Leadership and Democracy in Africa', Paper presented at UNESCO Conference on Ethnicity, Nationalism and Democracy in Africa, Kericho, Kenya, 28th-31st May.

Amutabi, M.N., and Were E.M., 2000, *Nationalism and Democracy for People-Centred Development in Africa*, Eldoret, Kenya, Moi University Press.

Barnett, D. L. and Njama, K., 1966, *Mau Mau From Within: Autobiography and Analysis of Kenya's Peasant Revolt*, London, MacGibbon & Kee.

Baxter, P. T. W., 1994, 'The Creation and Constitution of Oromo Nationality', in K. Fukui and J. Markakis (eds.), *Ethnicity and Conflict in the Horn of Africa*, London and Athens, James Currey and Ohio University Press, pp.167-186.

Baxter, P., 1979, 'Boran Age-sets and Warfare', in K. Fukui and D. Turton, (eds.), *Warfare among East African Herders*, Osaka, Senri Ethnological Foundation, National Museum of Ethnology.

Behnke, R.H., I. Scoones & C. Kerven, ed., 1993, *Range, Ecology at Disequilibrium: New Models of Natural Variability and Pastoral Adaptation in African Savannas*, London: Overseas Development Institute.

Clarence-Smith, W. G., 1979, Slaves, Peasants and Capitalists in Southern Angola, 1840-1926, Cambridge: Cambridge University Press.

Coppock, L., 1994, *The Borana Plateau of Southern Ethiopia: Synthesis of Pastoral Research, Development and Change, 1980-91*, Addis Ababa, International Livestock Centre for Africa (ILCA).

Crummey, D., 1986a, 'Introduction: "The Great Beast"', in Donald Crummey (ed.), *Banditry, Rebellion and Social Protest in Africa*, London and Portsmouth, New Hampshire: James Currey and Heinemann, pp.1-29.

Crummey, D., 1986b, 'Banditry and Resistance: Noble and Peasant in Nineteenth-Century Ethiopia', in Donald Crummey (ed.), *Banditry, Rebellion and Social Protest in Africa*, London and Portsmouth, New Hampshire: James Currey and Heinemann, pp.133-149.

Daily Nation, July 7, 2001, (Online Edition).

Dent, O. L., 1977, 'Manhood, Warrior-hood and Sex in Eastern Africa', in A. Mazrui (ed.), *The Warrior Tradition in Modern Africa*, Leiden, E.J Brill.

Fugich, W., 1999, 'The Role of Gada in Decision-Making and Its Implication for Pastoral Development and Poverty Alleviation among Borana', Paper presented at conference on community education co-hosted by Action-Aid and Association for World education (AWE), Isiolo, Kenya, August 25–28, 1999.

Fukui, K., 1994, 'Conflict and Ethnic Interaction: The Mela and their Neighbours', in K. Fukui and J. Markakis. (eds.), *Ethnicity and Conflict in the Horn of Africa*, London and Athens: James Currey and Ohio University Press, pp.33-47.

Fukui, K and D. Turton, eds., 1979, Warfare among East African Herders, Osaka, Senri, (nd.), Ethnological Foundation, National Museum of Ethnology.

Furedi, F., 1989, *The Mau Mau War In Perspective*, Nairobi, Heinemann.

Galaty, J.D., 1987, 'Form and Intention in East African Strategies of dominance', in D. McGuinnes, (ed.), *Dominance, Aggression and War*, New York: Paragon House Publishers.

Gufu, O., 1998, *Assessment of Indigenous Range Management Knowledge of Boran Pastoralists of Southern Ethiopia*, Neghelle, Report to the GTZ Boran Lowland Pastoral Development Program.

Helland, J., 1993, 'Institutional Erosion in the Drylands: The Case of the Borana Pastoralists', *Eastern Africa Social Science Review*, XIV, No.2. pp.21-32.

Hobsbawn, E.J., 1981, *Bandits,* Harmondsworth: Penguin, 2nd ed.

Kaggia, B., 1975, *Roots of Freedom*, Nairobi: East African Publishing House.

Kanogo, T., 1987, 'Kikuyu Women and the Politics of Mau Mau', in S. MacDonald et al. (eds.), *Images and Women in Peace and War: Cross-cultural Historical Perspectives*, London: Macmillan. pp.123-38.

Keller, E.J., 1973, 'A Twentieth Century Model: The Mau Mau Transformation from Social Banditry to Social Rebellion', *Kenya Historical Review*, 1, 2, 189-205.

Kinyatti, wa M. (ed.), 1986, *Kimathi's Letters: A Profile of Patriotic Courage*, Nairobi: Heinemann.

Kinyatti, wa M., 1980, *Thunder from the Mountains: Mau Mau Patriotic Songs*, Nairobi, Midi-Tera Publishers.

Lamphear, J., 1994, 'The Evolution of Ateker "New Model" Armies: Jie and Turkana', in K. Fukui and J. Markakis (eds.), *Ethnicity and Conflict in the Horn of Africa*, London and Athens: James Currey and Ohio University Press, pp.63-94.

Markakis, J., 1998, *Resource Conflict in the Horn of Africa*, London and New Delhi: Sage Publications.

Muller, H., 1989, *Changing Generations: Dynamics of Generation and Age-Sets in Southeastern Sudan (Toposa) and North-eastern Kenya (Turkana)*, Searbrucken: Breitenbach Publishers.

Nangulu-Ayuku, A., 2000, 'Politics, Urban Planning and Population Settlement, Nairobi, 1912-1916', *Journal of Third World Studies*, Vol. XVII, No.2, Fall, 171-204.

Nnoli, O. ,1998, 'Ethnic Conflicts in Eastern Africa', in O. Nnoli (ed.), *Ethnic Conflicts in Africa*, Dakar: CODESRIA.

Opondo, O., 2001, *Sunday Nation*, January 21, 2001.

Parker, G., 1988, *The Military Revolution*, Cambridge: Cambridge University Press.

Perner, C., 1993, "The Reward of Life is Death': Warfare and Anyuak of the Ethiopian-Sudanese Border', in T. Tvedt (ed.), *Conflicts in the Horn of Africa: Human and Ecological Consequences of Warfare*, Uppsala: Uppsala University, Department of Social and Economic Geography, pp.125-142.

Scoones, I., ed., 1995, *Living With Uncertainty: New Directions in Pastoral Development in Africa*, London, Intermediate Technology Publications.

Temu, A. J., 1972, *British Protestant Missions*, London: Longman.

Tornay, S. A., 1993, 'More Chances on the Fringe of the State? The Growing Power of the Nyangatom, a Border People of the Lower Omo Valley, Ethiopia (1970-1992)', in T. Tvedt (ed.), *Conflicts in the Horn of Africa: Human and Ecological Consequences of Warfare*, Uppsala: Uppsala University, Department of Social and Economic Geography, pp.143-163.

Turton, D., 1993, 'We Must Teach Them To Be Peaceful': Mursi Views on Being Human and Being Mursi', in T. Tvedt (ed.), *Conflicts in the Horn of Africa: Human and Ecological Consequences of Warfare*, Uppsala, Sweden, Uppsala University, Department of Social and Economic Geography, pp.164-180.

Turton, D., 1994, 'Mursi Political Identity and Warfare: The Survival of an Idea', in K. Fukui and J. Markakis (eds.), *Ethnicity and Conflict in the Horn of Africa*, London and Athens: James Currey and Ohio University Press, pp.15-32.

9

Legal and Political Dilemma in Transforming a Movement to Multi-Party System in Uganda: Is the National Resistance Movement Riding on a Tiger's Back?

Mohammed Kulumba

Introduction

> For many, however, hope seemed to momentarily resurface only to fizzle out again very much like a drowning person popping his or her head above the water surface before sinking once more in.
> – J. Oloka-Onyango, in *Law and the Struggle for Democracy in East Africa.*

Since 1986, when the National Resistance Movement (NRM) captured state power, Uganda has been governed under the Movement or 'No-Party' Political System. Any change to other political systems requires a referendum. However, recent legal and political developments have led the NRM to transform itself into a political party – an inevitable step, given the political behaviour of the regime in the almost two decades of its governance.

One of the legal developments is the landmark constitutional court ruling in the Semogerere and others vs Attorney General case. The ruling among others nullified sections 18 and 19 of the Political Parties and Organisations Act 2002 that barred political parties from active participation in the political process, and by implication setting them free. This development in a way forced some NRM loyalists to initiate a process of transforming the NRM into a political party.

We argue that the transformation of NRM from the Movement/No-Party system to a political party is as risky as riding on a tiger's back. This is especially so within the context of legal basis and Movement politics in the last 18 years, its background and original ideological orientations. We add that unless these fundamental issues are systematically and effectively addressed, Uganda may slip back into the political instability and violence that has characterised most of its entire post-independence period. Indeed at this point in history, Uganda is very much like a drowning person popping his or her head above the water surface before sinking once more. However it is not too late to save Uganda. Be it as it may, before any attempt at saving the life of this 'sinking person', we need to examine both the legal and political dilemma facing the NRM transition. We are guided among others by the following questions:

- Does the Political Party and Organisation Act 2002, contain sufficient legal framework to allow competitive multi-party politics in Uganda?

- What is the link and implication between the Constitutional Court ruling and the transformation of the NRM into a political party?

- Is it possible to have multi-partyism in a conflict situation in the North and North-Eastern part of Uganda?

- What will be the behaviour of the military in competitive multi-party system?

- Is there any contradiction between NRM Constitution and the Political Parties and Organisation Act 2002?

- Does the Political Parties and Organisations Act 2002 (PPOA) contain sufficient legal mechanisms to allow competitive multi-party politics?

- To what extent has the NRM involved the people of Uganda in its transformation?

This chapter is divided into three main sections. The first examines and interprets the legal basis and dilemma concerning the NRM transformation. The second section focuses on the political dilemma in the transformation. The third section contains some suggestions for the way forward and a conclusion.

Legal Basis and Dilemma Regarding NRM Transformation

The Constitutional Court Ruling

Background
As we have noted, the Constitutional Court ruling of 21st March 2003 set in motion a process of transforming the Movement into a political party. It is therefore desirable to revisit and examine the background, contents and implications of the ruling on the Uganda political process. The ruling was over a Constitutional Petition No. 5 of 2002, between Dr. Paul K. Semogerere and others (representing the supporters of Multi-Party system) and the Attorney General of Uganda. They were petitioning against sections 18 and 19 of the PPOA (2002). According to these sections:

• 18 (1) Notwithstanding anything in this Act, during the period when the Movement political system is in force, political activities may continue except that no Political Party or Organisation shall -

(a) Sponsor or offer a platform to, or in any way campaign for or against candidate in any Presidential or Parliamentary election or any other election organised by the Electoral Commission.

(b) Use any symbol, slogan, colour or name identifying any Political Party or organisation for the purpose of campaigning for, or against any candidate in any election referred to in the paragraph

(c) Open offices below the National Level.

(d) Hold public meetings, except for national Conferences, Executive Committee meetings, seminars and conferences held at the national level and the meetings referred to in subsection (7) and (8) of section 10 of this act.

• 18 (2) A Political Party or organisation shall not hold more than one national conference in a year. Any political party or organisation which contravenes this section commits an offence and -

(a) Is liable on conviction to a fine not exceeding three hundred currency points and

(b) Any member of the executive committee of a political party or organisation who contributes in any way to the contravention also commits the offence and is liable on conviction to a fine not exceeding three hundred currency points or imprisonment not exceeding three years or both.

• 19. Subject to clause (2) of Article 73 of the constitution, during the period when the Movement Political system is in force, and until another political system is adopted in accordance with the constitution, no organisation subscribing to any other political system shall carry on any activity that may interfere with the operation of the Movement political system.

The petition was placed before the Constitutional Court under Article 137 (3) of the 1995 constitution, which states that:

A person who alleges that:

(a) An Act of Parliament or any other law or any thing done under the authority of an law; or

(b) Any act or omission by any person or authority, is inconsistent with or in contravention of a provision of the constitution, may petition the constitution court for a declaration to that, and for redress where appropriate.

The petitioners therefore filed their petition challenging the constitutionality of section 18 and 19 of the Act on the following grounds, namely:

(a) That sections 18 and 19 of the Political Parties and Organisations Act of 2002 (hereinafter refer to as the Act) are inconsistent with articles 20, 29 (1), (a), (b), (c), and (e) and 2 (a); 43 (1) and 2 (c); 71; 73 (2) and 286 of the constitution and the various International Human Rights Conventions to which Uganda is a party, as they impose unjustifiable restrictions and limitations on the activities of Political Parties rendering them non functional and inoperative.

(b) That in contravention of Article 75 of the Constitution, sections 18 and 19 of the Act render Political Parties and Organisations non-functional and inoperative, thereby in effect establishing a one party state; namely the Movement.

(c) That in contravention of Article 21 of the Constitution, the Act is discriminatory in so far as it gives different treatments to different persons on the basis of their political opinion and inclination.

The petitioners argued that sections 18 and 19 of the PPOA (2002) impose unjustifiable restrictions or limitations on the activities of Political Parties and Organisation contrary to Article 73 (2) of the Constitution. According to this Article and section:

Regulations prescribed under this Article shall not exceed what is necessary for enabling the political system adapted to operate.

They further argued that sections 18 and 19 of the Act do render Political Parties and Organisations non-functional and inoperative. In addition, and most fundamentally for the multi-party system petitioners, that these sections 18 and 19 of the Act, in effect, establish a One Party State in favour of the Movement political organisation contrary to Article 75 of the constitution. According to this Article:

Parliament Shall Have no Power to Enact a Law Establishing a One-Party State

Constitutional Court Declarations

On 21 March 2003, the Constitutional Court unanimously agreed with petitioners' arguments and declared sections 18 and 19 of the PPOA null and void. They made the following declaration:

i) That sections 18 and 19 of the Political Parties and Organisation Act 2002 impose unjustifiable restrictions or limitations on the activities of Political Parties and Organisations contrary to Article 73 (2) of the constitution.

ii) That sections 18 and 19 of the Act do render Political Parties and Organisations non- functional and inoperative.

iii) That sections 18 and 19 of the Act, in effect, establish a One Party State in favour of the Movement Political Organisation contrary to Article 75 of the Constitution.

iv) That sections 18 and 19 are inconsistent with articles 20 (2), 29 (1) (d) and (e), 43 (1) and 2 (c) and 73 (2) of the Constitution. These sections are however not inconsistent with articles 20 (1), 29 (1) (a) (b) and 2 (a) of the Constitution.

v) That the International Human Rights Conventions mentioned in the petition are not part of the Constitution of the Republic of Uganda. Therefore, a provision of an Act of Parliament cannot be interpreted against them. They therefore declared sections 18 and 19 null and void.

We highlight here some of the reasons and arguments advanced by the Judges to justify their declarations. These we believe are important in examining the legal dilemma in the Movement transformation to a Political Party. Their reasons and arguments were intended to address the following questions derived from the petition.

1) Whether or not sections 18 and 19 of the Political Parties and Organisations Act impose unjustifiable restrictions or limitations on the activities of Political Parties and organisations?

2) Whether or not sections 18 and 19 of Political Parties and Organisations Act render Political Parties and organisations non- functional and inoperative?

3) Whether sections 18 and 19 of the Political Parties and Organisations Act are inconsistent with Article 75 of the Constitution and establish a One Party State; the party being the Movement?

4) Whether or not sections 18 and 19 of the Act are inconsistent with articles 20, 29 (1) (a), (b), (d) and (e) and 2 (a), 43(1) and 2 (c), 71,73(2) and 286 of the constitution?

5) Whether sections 18 and 19 of the Act contravene the International Human Rights Conventions mentioned in the petition and if so, whether that makes the Sections unconstitutional?

6) Whether or not the Act is discriminatory, contrary to Article 21 of the constitution?

Response to Questions 1 and 2

In response to these questions, the Judges argued that the essence of a political party as defined by section 2 of the Act is to be able, among other things, to sponsor or offer a platform to candidates for election to a political office and participation in the governance of the country at any level. Similarly, a political organisation should be able to influence the political process or sponsor a political agenda, whether or not it also seeks to sponsor or offer a platform to a candidate for election to a political office or to participate in the governance of the country at any level.

They noted that all these essential attributes of political parties and organisations are exactly what the restrictions under sections 18 and 19 target, by prohibiting them from sponsoring or offering the platform for, or against a candidate in Presidential or Parliamentary elections, or any other election organised by the Electoral Commission; use of symbols, slogans, colour or name identifying any political party or organisation for the purpose of campaigning for, or against a candidate; opening offices below national level, holding public meetings and not to hold more than one national conference in a year. They argued that denying these roles to other political parties and organisations is tantamount to extinguishing them, thus leaving them to exist, but in name. They stated that the reasons given by the respondent (Attorney General) to justify the restrictions were purely anticipatory and speculative. They observed that an attempt was made to justify the restrictions on the grounds of the past violent history of political parties and their devastating effect on the rule of law. They argued that with due respect, the past violence of the parties is irrelevant to the constitutional validity of the impugned sections 18 and 19. They observed that while courts do guard against a return to such past violence (De Clerk and Another Vs Du Plesses and Athers [Supra]), the Constitution has to be construed in the context, scene and setting that exists at the time when the interpretation has to be determined. Most importantly, it was acknowledged by some witnesses; Hon. Wapahabulo, Mr. Nadduli and Odola Oryem, that people do change with time. Evidence emerged that political parties per se are not violent. People constitute the parties. Parties therefore do change and have been proved not to be a preserve of violence and divisionism.

The restrictions were therefore proved unjustifiable and were found to render the political parties and organisations inoperative. This state of affairs in the view of Honourable judges may eventually lead to total extinction of political parties. While the judges acknowledged the respondents' essential goals of the maintenance of unity and stability in the country, they argued that it was equally important to recognise the preservation of individual rights in an achieving those goals. The judges therefore answered questions 1 and 2 in affirmative.

Response to Question 3

The Honourable judges established that the Movement is a political organisation with all the attributes of a political organisation. It has a symbol of the yellow bus. It intends to acquire property and set up its headquarters. It vies for power. It urges or sponsors candidates openly to stand for elections. This, they noted, was more amplified by a circular dated 10 May 2001 on Guidance on Parliamentary Elections from the Movement Chairman, where the Movement loyalists were being urged to select one strong candidate and rally behind him/her for election against the Multi-Partyists. It is able to traverse the country down to the grassroots advocating its political views.

As pointed out under question 1 and 2, by assuming all the attributes and functions of a political party while at the same time denying them to other parties and organisations, the Movement was making it clear that it intended to remain the only organisation in the political arena with no competitor subscribing to alternative views. This would not require any specific law enacted as contended by the respondents.

The spirit is discernible throughout the Constitution that its framers intended that people should always have political parties. The right to form political parties and any other political organisation is guaranteed under Article 72 (1). Hence they argued that the inclusion of Article 75, which prohibits Parliament from enacting a law to establish a One-Party State. Parties existed before the promulgation of 1995 constitution. They were never banned, but they were preserved thereunder, albeit severely restricted, under the transitional Article 269 until suitable guidelines for their operation and functions could be made, and which were made under the Act. It was clear, however, that since the parties had been nonfunctional since 1995, the effect of the restrictions under the Act on them would hasten their eventual demise rather than reform them. They argued therefore, that they cannot reform without being active, convening regular meetings, seminars and conferences generally, and mobilising members from the national and down to the grassroots as the Movement is actively engaged in doing.

The evidence clearly indicated that the effect of the restrictions in sections 18 and 19 established a One Party State contrary to Article 75. They therefore answered the question in the affirmative.

Response to Question 4

Article 20 provides:

1) Fundamental Rights and freedoms of individual are inherent and not granted by the State.

2) The rights and freedoms of individual and groups enshrined within the Chapter shall be respected, upheld and promoted by all organs and agencies of government and by all persons.

They observed that Parliament being an organ of the Government, passed section 18 and 19 of the Act, which have been proved to violate the petitioners' fundamental rights and freedoms of assembly and association. This is in conflict with, and is inconsistent with the principle under Article 20 (2) which provides that these rights are inherent and are not granted by the State, and cannot therefore be taken away or withdrawn by the State or any organ thereof, let alone any individual except in the specified way under Article 43. They concluded that the rationale behind Chapter Four in the Constitution is to constantly remind the Government that these are important and special rights and freedoms necessary for the preservation of a free and democratic society, and which have to be abridged in the specified way therein contained.

Regarding Article 29, which protects the freedom of conscience, expression movement, religion, assembly and association, they noted that the claim of violation of Article 29 (1) (a), (b) and 2 (a) was not supported by evidence. However, Article 29 (1) (d) and (e) as a subject of this petition provides as follows:

29 (1) Every person shall have a right to -

(a) Freedom to assemble and demonstrate together with others peacefully and unarmed to petition, and

(b) Freedom of association, which shall include the freedom to form and join associations or unions, including Trade Unions and Political and other Civic organisations.

They noted that the freedoms to assemble and associate, in as far as this petition is concerned, do not only concern the right to form a political party, but also guarantee the right of such a party once formed to carry on its political activities freely. Such an association is a highly effective means of communication. It stimulates public discussion and debate of the issues concerning the country, often offering constructive criticism of government programmes and alternative use. The right to freedom of association lies at the very foundation of a democratic society, and is one of the basic or core conditions for its progress and development. They concluded that the restrictions in sections 18 and 19 were therefore inconsistent with Article 29 (1) (d) and (e).

Concerning Article 33, the judges argued that it placed a general limitation on the enjoyment of the fundamental rights and freedoms. Any limitation on these rights and freedoms must conform to what is acceptable and justifiable under a democratic society or what is provided in the Constitution, as pointed out earlier in this judgement. It had been established that the Movement was a political organisation and not a system as purportedly envisaged under Article 73 (1). That being so, they further argued that the restrictions on the petitioners' fundamental rights and freedoms have to be tested under Article 43 (2) (c) to see whether they complied with what is acceptable and demonstrably justifiable in a free and democratic society or what is provided in this Constitution. They noted that it has been shown by evidence that sections 18 and 19 have excessively eroded the petitioners' rights and freedoms of assembly and association. To that extent, the sections are inconsistent with Article 43 (2) (c). The respondent failed to justify the restrictions under Article 73 (2) in that they far exceed what is necessary for the Movement to operate.

As to whether sections 18 and 19, contravene Article 20 and 86 of the Constitution, they were of the opinion that these Articles preserve and save Treaties, Agreements or Conventions to which Uganda was a party before coming into effect of the 1995 Constitution. They therefore concluded that the Article does not make them part of the Constitution and hence they could not interpret provisions of an Act of Parliament against them.

Finally, regarding whether the Act is discriminatory contrary to Article 21 of the Constitution, they argued that counsel never addressed it. They therefore could not offer opinion on it.

Link and Implications Between the Constitutional Court Ruling and the NRM Transformation

To begin with, we must take into account the reality as expounded in the Constitutional Court Ruling that a Constitution must be interpreted in the context, scene and setting that exists at the time when the interpretation has to be determined and not when it was promulgated. Otherwise, it would cease to take into account the growth of society it seeks to regulate and ignore the future implications and impact of the sound construction on future generations. For this reason, courts do breath life into the constitution, bearing in mind that it is neither a 'lifeless museum peace' nor is it frozen, but is organic and it grows. This was clearly articulated by Lord Wright in the Australian case of James V Commonwealth of Australia (1936) AC 518 at 614 (Semogerere vs Attorney General Court Ruling, p. 11).

Put differently, the court ruling laid down cardinal principles that would guide the political development of the country. However, the founders of the proposed National Resistance Movement Political Organisation (NRM-O) appear not to have grasped the spirit and wisdom in this court ruling. For example, it was explicitly pointed out by the judges as we noted, 'that the Movement was a political organisation. It is defined by its deeds and actions. It vies for power. It has a symbol, which is normally associated with Political Parties. It can sponsor candidates to stand for elections thus flouting the principle of individual merit'.

What was the implication of this ruling for the nature and form of the NRM? The implications were many. First it meant that whereas it was the desire of the framers of the 1995 Ugandan Constitution to put in place a 'Movement' political system, its practicability soon thereafter was one of a political party or organisation. Indeed a number of scholars have testified to this reality. For example, Mugaju and Oloka Onyango (2000:2) argue that:

.... no party democracy is simply one-party dictatorship by another name and also constitutes a ban of the right to organise opposition. The pretence of 'broad-based inclusiveness' was deliberately designed by the NRM leadership to monopolise power at the expense of other political forces in the country.

It therefore followed that since NRM had been in existence as a political organisation since 1986, one cannot overnight begin a process of transforming it into what it already was. There is thus the illegality contestation to the process of transforming NRM into a political organisation within the context of the constitutional court ruling.

Since, there was a *prima facie* case that the NRM was a political organisation, its loyalists with a desire for participation in a competitive multi-Party system, that requires registration of a political party under the Political Parties and Organisations Act 2002, would have started this process under the guidance of the Movement Act, 1997. The Movement Act, in addition to regulating the functioning of the Movement, provides under Article 4 that (1) the Movement National Conference is the highest organ under the Movement. In addition, under 10 (1), and 11 (1), the Act provides for the National Executive Committee (NEC) with the following functions:

a) Initiate policy and other measures considered by the National Conference

b) Deal with policy matters on behalf of the National Conference

c) Be responsible for the day-to-day affairs of the conference

d) Advise the National Conference on the performance of its functions; and

e) Perform other functions as the National Conference may direct.

Indeed, for the process of registering the NRM-O (Movement) to have had legality, it should have been undertaken by the NEC under Article 11 (e) of the Movement Act. Since neither the National Conference of the Movement nor NEC were consulted, and consented to the registration of NRM-O under the Political Parties and Organisation Act 2002, the whole process is null and void.

To highlight the legal dilemma facing the transformation of the NRM into a Political Organisation, we now examine some of the sections of its Constitution, the provisions of the Political Party and Organisations Act and the 1995 Constitution. We believe by doing so, the dilemma will be much clearer. We must remind ourselves of the following questions to guide our discussion:

• To what extent do the provisions of Political Parties and Organisations Act guarantee competitive multi-party practices in Uganda?

• Does the NRM-O constitution conform to constitutional order, rules and procedures?

• To what extent does the NRM transformation conform to the constitutional framework and legal regimes in the country?

• What were the intentions of the NRM loyalists in initiating the transformation process?

As we have noted, the response of some NRM loyalists to the Constitutional Court ruling was to set in motion processes towards transforming the Movement into a political organisation. One of the processes was to prepare a constitution for the 'New Political Organisation'. We now examine some of the provisions of NRM-O constitution together with the existing legal framework.

Under chapter 2 of the NRM-O constitution for Vision, Mission Character, Aims and Objectives, Article 6 (1) states that 'NRM is a national, broad-based, inclusive, democratic, non-sectarian, multi- ideological, multi-interests and pro-gressive mass organisation.' Similarly, according to Article 70 (1) of the 1995 Constitution that defines the Movement system; the Movement political system is broad-based, inclusive and non-partisan.

It is quite clear that the promoters of NRM-O merely reproduced the Move-ment as defined and provided for under the 1995 Constitution of Uganda and incorporated the same provisions into the NRM-O constitution. But more fun-damentally, the action can be subjected to legal contestations. Firstly, it contra-venes Article 74 (1) of the 1995 Constitution, which expressly states that a refer-endum shall be held for purposes of changing a political system. Put differently, the desire to transform a Movement into a political organisation would have been put to a referendum vote, following the spirit of these constitutional provi-sions for the process to be legally acceptable. We are aware of Article 74 (2) of the 1995 constitution that provides for a change of a political system by parlia-ment and district councils. However, although the Constitutional Review Com-mission concluded its work and recommended a return to multi-party pluralism, there is no programme to date to involve the districts in the debates over chang-ing the political system. Indeed what is happening confirms the observation of Oloka Onyango (2000: 505), that:

> The NRM record on constitutionalism in its own interim period speaks volumes about the sustainability of the constitutional order that it seeks to create. The NRM, which promised to be merely the midwife to ensure a safe delivery, is now active like a mother that wants to determine the sex of the child. Because Yoweri Museveni is no Aquino, i.e. committed to the transfer of power rather than to retain it at all costs, the ultimate conclu-sion that must be made is that the transition process is coloured by the fact that the NRM wants to have its cake and to eat it!

To be exact, this is another case of 'Constitutional gymnastics or engineering' common to many regimes in Africa that have of recent painfully and forcibly embarked on the delicate and complex process of constitutional order in a state.

Secondly, the illegality of the NRM transformation can be observed when one critically examines some of the provisions of the PPOA 2002. For example, according to Article 2:

> 'The definition of 'Political Organisation' in subsection (1) shall not in-clude the following; The Movement political system referred to in Article 70 of the constitution and the organs and the movement political system'. Under Article (1) of the constitution of NRM-O, the name of the or-ganisation shall be 'The National Resistance Movement', hereinafter re-ferred to as NRM. It is well documented to the effect that since the legal notice No. 1 of 1986, which laid down the legal basis of the Movement system in Uganda, it has been referred to as NRM. For this reason, the

Movement system in Uganda is known and goes by the name of NRM. Therefore, to adopt a known and officially recognised name for the Movement system by a new political party no doubt will be legally contested, since Article 2 (2) outlaws or forbids the definition or name of an organisation to include the Movement political system.

One may wonder why the promoters of NRM-O did not think of another name other than the NRM that conflicts with the provisions of the Political Parties and the Organisations Act 2002. One may argue that the intentions of the promoters of NRM-O were essentially to hoodwink the unsuspecting peasants into believing that the NRM-O was indeed the historical NRM political system. This would inevitably ensure political support of peasants that still cherish the ideal of the historical Movement political system, thus giving NRM-O an advantage over other political parties in a competitive multi-party election.

Thirdly, the illegality of NRM-O can also be seen in its colours and symbol as described under Schedule 1 of the party's Constitution. The colours of NRM-O are a combination of blue, yellow, red and green. While the symbol of NRM is a combination of a yellow bus, thumbs up and open book. The position of the law as established in Semogerere and others, is very clear on this matter. It was declared that: 'The Movement is a political organisation with all attributes of a political organisation. It has a symbol of a yellow bus'.

Be that as it may, the essence here is that the NRM-O cannot use colours and symbols of an already existing political organisation (the NRM). This illegality in using symbols and colours similar to the existing political organisation is equally spelled out in the Political Parties and Organisation Act 2002, under article 8. It states:

No political party or organisation shall submit to the Registrar General for the purpose of registration under section 7 of this Act, in identifying symbol, slogan, colour or name, which is the same as, or similar to the symbol, slogan, colour or name or initials of -

a) any registered Political Party or organisation; or

b) any existing political party or organisation continued in existence under article 270 of the constitution; or

c) the Republic of Uganda; or

d) statutory co-operation or other body the whole or the greater part of the proprietary interest in which is held by or on behalf of the state; or in which the state has a controlling interest; or

e) which so closely resemble the symbol, slogan, colour or name or initials of another political party or organisation or the Republic of Uganda, or a body described in the paragraph (d) as to be likely to deceive or confuse members of the public.

The legal dilemma of NRM-O is also reflected in its organs. Under Chapter Four of its constitution (Organs of NRM) Article 10 (1), it states that NRM-O shall have the following organs:

(a) Policy Organs

    (i) The National Conference

    (ii) The National Executive Council

    (iii) Etc.

(b) Administrative Organs

    (i) The National Secretariat

    (ii) The District Executive Committees

    (iii) Etc.

(c) Special Organs

    (i) NRM historical leaders Forum

    (ii) The Women League

    (iii) The Youth League...

    (iv) The NRA and UPDF Veterans League.

There are two main legal issues here, which we must point out in relation to NRM-O organs as stipulated under Article 10(1) of its constitution. First, like the previous sections and subsections of NRM-O constitution, this one too was directly reproduced from the Movement Act. For example, under Article 4 (1) of the Movement Act 1997, it states:

> The Movement shall have a National Conference, which shall be the highest organ under the Movement.

Similarly, Article 4 (2) stipulates the organs under the Movement are as follows:

    (a) The National Executive Committee

    (b) The Secretariat of the Movement

    (c) District Movement Committees

Secondly, but most fundamentally, the NRM-O proposes 'The National Resistance Army (NRA) and Uganda People Defence Forces (UPDF) veterans, as one of its special organs. We must point out that these veterans are part of the UPDF administration under 'Reserve Forces' complete with a command structure. Indeed, the reserve force has been deployed from time to time to participate in military missions along with UPDF. Therefore their inclusion in political party organs is illegal under existing legal framework.

The PPOA 2002 is explicit on participation of military personnel in political party activities. Under Article 16(1):

A member of Uganda People's Defence Forces, the Uganda Police Force, Uganda Prisons Service or public officer or a traditional or cultural leader shall not:

   a) be a founding member or other members of the political party or organisation; or

   b) hold office in a political party or organisation; or

   c) speak in public or publish anything involving matters of political party or organisation controversy; or

   d) engage in conversing in support of a political party or organisation or of a candidate standing for public election sponsored by political party or organisation.

This discussion has attempted to answer some of the issues raised at the beginning of this subsection. To conclude this subsection therefore, we now turn to the question: 'To what extent do the provisions of Political Parties and Organisation Act guarantee competitive Multi-Party politics in the country?'

To begin with, the Political Parties and Organisation Act 2002 aims at regulating the financing and functioning of political parties and organisations, their registration, membership and organisation pursuant to Articles 72 and 73 of the 1995 constitution. It is our contention that the Act in general is a bad law, which was made in bad faith and ill will against political parties. In that context it cannot guarantee a fair and competitive multi-party system in the country, unless of course the law courts gives it 'major surgery' as they did in relation to its sections 18 and 19 during the Semogerere and Others vs. Attorney General Constitutional Court ruling. We examine some of its provisions to justify our contention.

Under Article 7 (1b), an application to register a political party or organisation shall be made to the Registrar General and shall be accompanied by:

A list of the full names and addresses of at least 50 members of the political party or organisation from each of at least one third of all the districts of Uganda, being members ordinarily resident or registered as voters in the district.

It is apparent that this Article was intended to stop the emergence of new political parties and to incapacitate the old ones; the Democratic Party (DP) and Uganda Peoples Congress (UPC). It is almost impossible for a new party to succeed in recruiting 50 representatives from each of at least half of the districts in Uganda to be able to register and compete in presidential and parliamentary election scheduled to take place in the year 2006. It is even more complicated in the context where many of the multi-party loyalists had in the past boycotted registration for participation in the NRM-organised elections. Indeed, this Article gives an advantage to NRM-O ahead of others, since older political parties, having been dormant in the last 18 years, would find it difficult to reactivate their membership or recruit new ones countrywide. These same phenomena occurred in Tanzania. According to Tambila (1996:30):

Twenty-seven years of one-party rule between 1965 and 1991, dominated by an all-embracing state party, critically crippled the creative capacity of the people to form their own organisations and manage them. Civil society was demobilised and controlled by the state party. It is proving to be a very tortuous experience to start afresh to create new democratic organisations after the almost 30 years of demobilisation.

This explains why in Uganda, despite the fact that twenty political parties and organisations picked up forms for registration under the Act, many were finding it difficult to register.

Similarly under the same Article 7 (1b):

an application to register the Political Party or organisation shall be made to the Registrar General and shall be accompanied by two copies of the constitution of the political party or organisation duly signed by author-ised officers of the political party organisation.

This subsection no doubt was also directed at the old political parties; that is the UPC and DP. For example, the UPC at the time of making this law had two factions. One headed by the President of the UPC National Policy Commission, Dr Rwanyarare, with the blessing of the exiled founding President, Dr. Apollo Milton Obote. Hon. Cecilia Ogwal headed the other. It is difficult to tell which of the two factions legally represented the interests of the UPC, thus qualifying it to proceed with registration under the Act. The DP too is bedevilled with similar factional problems.

Another legal complication is to be found under Article 13 of PPAO 2002 Act. It states that no person shall be appointed nor accept any political office in a Political Party or organisation in Uganda, if he or she: 'has, immediately before he or she is to be appointed, lived outside Uganda continuously for more than three years'.

This provision targeted several leaders of political parties and civic organisa-tions who, at the time of making this law were living in exile, from competing with NRM-O in a competitive multi-party system. One example is Dr. Kizza Besigye, the leader of the Reform Agenda, a pressure group which is demanding reforms in NRM, and who effectively competed with President Museveni during the 2001 Presidential Elections.

It is a well-established tradition that political parties and organisations mobi-lise financial resources for the purpose of running a party, including for example sponsoring candidates for election to political office and participation in the gov-ernance of the country at any level. Indeed in competitive multi-party systems this exercise is very instrumental for the success of political parties in an election. The most successful political party in an election would in most cases be one that surpassed above others in mobilising financial resources, especially from the business community and other powerful interest groups. However, under Article 9 (3) of PPAO Act: 'Every political party or organisation must submit to the Registrar General the sources of funds and other assets of the political party or organisation'.

This provision appears to have been intended to target older political parties, and to cripple them financially. The reality is that no business people will be willing to finance a political party only to be ostracised by the state. This is important in the Ugandan context in the sense that in the majority of cases, the success or failure of most business enterprises depends on the patronage of the state by way of government contracts and so on. Similarly, in the event that the source of finance for a political party is from another state, this may lead to diplomatic conflict or tensions between the ruling party and the state involved in funding a rival political party. This is especially so when a financing state is known to have an interest in influencing political developments in the state.

Article 14 (1 and 2) of the same Act makes the financial positions of political parties and other organisations even more precarious. It states that:

1. The following shall not directly or indirectly make a contribution, donation or loan whether in cash or kind in excess of the value of five thousands currency points within any period of 12 months, to funds held or to be held by or for the benefits of a political party or organisation:

    (a) a non-Ugandan Citizen;

    (b) a foreign Government or Diplomatic Mission;

    (c) a non-Ugandan Non-Governmental Organisation registered in Uganda under the Non- Governmental Organisations Registration Statute, 1989.

2. No political party or organisation shall-

    (a) Demand or accept directly or indirectly any contribution, donation or loan in excess of the value of five thousand currency points within any period of 12 months, from any organisation specified in subsection (1) of this section; or

    (b) Demand or accept directly or indirectly any contribution, donation or loan in excess of the total value of fifty thousand currency points in any period of 12 months from anyone or more of the sources referred to in subsection (1).

It is indeed unfortunate that such an unfair and unjust law can be passed in a state legislature. This is especially so given that Uganda's recent economic success is largely linked to the massive financial support from western governments, donor agencies, institutions and NGOs. This has been mainly in the form of direct and indirect financial contributions, donations, loans, grants and, recently, debt relief (Kulumba 2003a:56).

To date, financial support from non-Ugandan NGOs is even included and reflected in the national and local government administration budgets. Indeed it is difficult to envisage the economic growth and development of national and local governments without NGO support. If this is the case, then why deny political parties and organisations the same? This is especially so within the context of the world being a 'global village'! Should the DP for example abandon its old link with the Global Coalition of the Christian Democratic Parties where it has benefited immensely, especially in financial terms?

Some answers to these questions may be found within the debates and arguments advanced by scholars and political analysts in relation to the Movement/NRM political system, in theory and practice. During the early and later days of the regime, they had quite clearly pointed out its intentions and limitations as a vehicle for a democratic political system. The NRM loyalists for their part have put up a strong argument against political parties right from the early days in the bush. Central to this thesis is their argument that political parties divide the people and cannot hold a nation together in a pre-industrialised and third world society with a peasant majority like Uganda. Mujaju (1996:24) dismisses this argument by asserting that:

> Tanzania is a proof that parties can work well in Third World Countries. TANU and CCM in Tanzania have been important bedrocks of the Tanzania polity. In India, the second largest peasant nation (China is the first), is held together by the Congress Party. Undoubtedly, without the Congress Party, India could very easily have broken apart many years. Malawi has started very well on the road to multi-partyism.

Mujaju concludes by advising what he calls 'the excited NRM Marxist' to forget many of these Marxist concepts (Movement/No Party system), and give people their legitimate rights to run their parties or form new ones. Put differently, it was theoretically and practically wrong for NRM loyalists to persist with theories that have been invalidated by such abundant evidence. One may therefore argue that the NRM transformation to a political organisation was an 'internal evolution' or mechanism to continue their hold on power. That is why they instituted such legal mechanisms to incapacitate the evolution of competitive political party pluralism in Uganda.

Mugaju and Oloka-Onyango (2000:2) observe that:

> ... the no-party democracy is a negation of the fundamental Human Rights of Association. That the no-party democracy is simply one-party dictatorship by another name and also constitutes a ban of the right to organised opposition. It is a convenient contrivance, which despite the pretence of broad-based inclusiveness was deliberately designed by the

NRM leadership to monopolise power at the expense of other political forces in the country.

Oloka-Onyango (1996) adds that contrary to what its proponents claim, the 'no-party' Movement system is neither unique nor is it an exemplary expression of the democratic ideal. According to him, Movement democracy is nothing more than the guided democracy of old in which political expression is both dictated and suppressed by the ruling political organisation of the day. But since by the 1980s, 'one-partyism' has fallen into disgrace, so it was conveniently repackaged in 'new bottles' and rebranded 'Movement', to lend it credibility both within and outside Uganda. He argues that the Movement politics has failed to eliminate the problems of ethnicity, religious sectarianism and corruption that multi-party systems are often accused of. Indeed, he asserts that 'the suffocation of democratic opposition in the country today makes even the possibility of the military coup d'état a very real one'.

Drawing on a wide theoretical and historical perspective, Barya (2000:25) examines the case for and against multi-partyism and the justification for the emergence of the no-party Movement political system in Uganda. Barya analyses the issues in the referendum debate between the multi-partyists and the Movementists and proposes what needs to be done to construct a political system acceptable to all forces across the political spectrum. He argues that the principle of Multi-partyism and the Movement are mutually exclusive and that the Movement's achievements can be adequately protected by a plural political arrangement that recognises Multi-partyism but avoids the pitfalls of winner-takes-all politics. At the same time, he warns of the dangers inherent in pursuing the referendum option, not simply in terms of the political context but also with regard to social and economic problems.

Clearly, from the theoretical and practical context and reality, the Movement Political system/NRM had reached a crossroad by 2002, when the Political Parties and Organisation Act was passed by Parliament. And given the political behaviour of the NRM and its inherent desire to keep state power through whatever legal and political means that has been well documented by scholars and analysed in this chapter, it was indeed not surprising for its transformation process to end in numerous illegalities.

We conclude this sub-section by noting that so far, NRM has succeed to register under PPAO Act 2002 despite the conflict and contradictions with the existing legal framework which we have examined. To that extent we argue that we are likely to witness in future more constitutional and court battles over NRM's transformation for a long period of time.

Political Dilemma of NRM's Transformation

There are several political dilemmas involved in the transformation of the NRM. These include NRM ideology, opposition from NRM historicals, the Northern Question, the role of the military, and co-operation among political parties.

NRM Ideological Incoherence

Mujaju (1996: 9) defines ideology as 'a body of ideas, which has action consequence, which contains a critique of existing reality and a view of the desired future, complete with a programme of achieving that future'. Does the NRM have an ideology? If it does, in which ways does it pose a dilemma for its transformation? The NRM can be said to have had an ideology at least in its formative years, though there have been a lot of inconsistencies in its orientation as it struggled to keep its dominance over state power. This ideology was embedded in the 'NRM Ten Point Programme', which was later expanded to fifteen points. Central to the NRM ideology, as we have noted in this chapter, is the 'Movement System of Governance' where membership is open to all regardless of political affiliation, religion, ethnicity or region. It has a complete programme to achieve this, through for example elections both at national and local levels conducted on the basis of 'Individual Merit'. We must add that the ideology also does not allow political parties to participate in a political process. For the purpose of this subsection, we are not examining the merits and demerits of NRM ideology. We have done this elsewhere (Kulumba 2001:3). However, we must note that NRM has been steadily 'selling' its ideology to the Ugandan community through programmes such as political education courses. During these courses, political parties are associated with the governance crisis in Uganda by NRM cadres. Mamdani (1993:43), for example, sums up the NRM critique of political parties in Uganda as follows:

> Small coteries of professional politicians, whose primary interest is to secure positions and privilege for themselves, often at the expense of the society as large. They tend to organise support not on the basis of a 'principled' discussion of issues and policies, but through an 'opportunistic' manipulation of divisive issues like religion and ethnicity. Elections and campaigns are not a time for them to educate and unite people along 'National Lines', but yet another opportunity to divide them along 'sectarian' lines. Their support base is not a membership that can hold the leadership accountable, but more of a bandwagon of followers that has little control or influence over the leadership. There is little that is democratic about the internal life of these state parties. As such, political parties in Uganda are more an obstacle to democratisation than a vehicle for it.

Is this summary of attributes of political parties in Uganda limited only to the political parties per se? Is it not true that these attributes are indeed a result of social, political and economic situations with a direct linkage to the nature of colonial and post-colonial politics in Uganda? Isn't the NRM guilty too of these vices? Most of these questions have been answered in affirmative in previous subsections of this chapter.

Another notable measure by the NRM to implement its ideology was the creation of the institution of Resistance Councils and Committees (RCs) that later became Local Councils (LCs) in the governance of the country. Indeed, according to Byarugaba (1997:47):

> Most people agree that a fundamental change has taken place in Ugandan politics since 1986. It is almost a miracle that RCs can today apprehend an Army Officer for questioning whom they find staying illegally in their area. In the past, the army was 'untouchable'. The RCs have a right to resist the Police from arresting a suspect in their areas without their consent. Furthermore, decision making has improved due to effective communication between the people and the various levels of RCs. Bureaucratic bottlenecks have been removed by RCs who have power in their hands.

We must add, that the NRM ideology has been well received especially by the majority of the rural people. In particular, older generation that witnessed the governance crisis associated with multi-party politics. Under these circumstances where NRM has succeeded in the last two decades in establishing a formidable alliance with peasants, notably over poor governance associated with political parties, we believe it is going to be difficult for the NRM to convince them to change and support the NRM's 'new clothes' of a political party. The NRM for this reason and because of its ideological inconsistencies will have to do a lot of groundwork in order to succeed. This certainly will require a lot of time.

Another notable political dilemma in the NRM transformation is a section of NRM historicals, who have authoritatively opposed the process. According to Sabiiti (1996:100), 'although Museveni usually says that he has no permanent friends and enemies, he has shown that he values friends who prove to be useful in the struggle. One such valuable life-friend is Eriya Kategaya. Together with other close friends, they launched a political struggle at a very tender age'. Already, President Museveni has relieved Eriya Kategaya of his Deputy Premiership and Ministerial Post of Internal Affairs due to his opposition to the current political developments in the Movement. The same befell Mr. Jaberi Bidandisali, also a long time friend of President Museveni with whom they founded the Uganda Patriotic Movement in 1980. It is difficult to tell the future actions of these two powerful men who, until recently, were the main architects of NRM governance and ideology. Indeed their departure from the NRM is a big blow to its transformation since they combine seniority in public administration and support from a large constituency, especially within the political elite.

The Northern Question

Gingera- Pinycwa (1992:3) notes that 'In the internal conflict that have bedevilled the political history of Uganda, since independence, Northern Uganda has largely featured as the black sheep, or may be even more accurately, as a bull in a china shop, wrecking and spoiling all that come in its way'. When NRM captured state power in 1986, conflict and violence broke out in the North and North-Eastern part of the country. Since then, thousands of ordinary people have lost their lives and property. Many have been displaced from their homes and villages and live in 'refugee life in camps' in their country. The war in the northern and north-eastern part of the country still persists. One wonders whether the Kony rebels fighting in the north and north-eastern part of the country are fighting the NRM regime or the Ugandan State in revenge for the historical injustices meted out to the peoples in these regions (Kulumba 2003a:285). The evidence on the ground seems to indicate that the rebels are fighting the NRM regime and not the Ugandan State. The Kony Lords Resistance Army (LRA) always observes cease-fires in the period preceding Presidential elections in the hope that a new and perhaps friendly government would be elected to replace the NRM. As it has usually turned out, they resume fighting the moment NRM is declared the winner. Indeed it has been pointed out that the LRA is fighting the NRM because of its monolithic political system that does not allow competitive politics in the country. Put differently, the LRA is fighting to reinstate a multi-party system in Uganda. So, what will be the response of the LRA to the NRM transformation into a political party organisation? Will Ugandans be assured of a future in which people do not hunt each other like animals in civil war and strife? Will multi-party politics succeed in the conflict situation prevailing in the country? We argue that the behaviour of the LRA is not likely to change by NRM's transformation into NRM-O, since the latter is constituted largely by the same members. Perhaps any change in northern Uganda politics can come about if NRM-O initiates new policy actions that differ fundamentally from the historical NRM.

The Role of the Military

The military has been an active player in the chequered political history of Uganda. The Uganda army was at the centre stage during the 1966 crisis when, led by Army Commander Idi Amin, 'smoked' out the first President of Uganda and the Kabaka (king) of Buganda, Sir Edward Mutesa, from his palace. The Kabaka managed to escape but later died in exile in 1969. The military under the same command deposed President Milton Obote in 1971.

During the NRM's tenure since 1986 it has been difficult to separate the NRA/Uganda Peoples Defence Forces (UPDF) from Movement system. This is not unique to the NRM, but is also true of all 'Liberation Movements' that have captured state power in Africa. President Yoweri Museveni is not only a Commander in chief of the UPDF, but an active officer with a rank of Lieutenant General (although he retired recently allegedly to head the NRM-O). He is known to spend months commanding his troops at war fronts. In such a context, one wonders about the behaviour of the military in a post-Movement period under a competitive multi-party system. This is particularly so in the event that the NRM-O is defeated by another party in a national election. Indeed during the 2001 presidential elections, according to Obongo-Oula: '…the then Minister of State for Security Col. Kahinda Otafire announced publicly that if any other candidate apart from Museveni won the Presidential elections, he would be overthrown within 24 hours' (2001:20).

Such statements and many others by senior officers of the UPDF put to question the sustainability of the NRM transformation and competitive multi-party democracy in Uganda.

Co-operation Between Political Parties

In a competitive multi-party system, it is desirable for political parties to cooperate amongst themselves. In some situations, political parties need the support of each other in order to offer a strong challenge to the ruling party. The Kenya National Rainbow Coalition (NARC) experience is a perfect example of such type of co-operation that defeated President Moi's KANU government (Kulumba 2003a:1). Similarly, during the 2001 Presidential elections in Uganda, the DP and UPC formed an alliance and supported one candidate, Dr. Semogerere, who competed with the NRM President Y. K. Museveni. However, given the tensions, suspicions and conflicts that have characterised NRM-political party relations, it is difficult to envisage a cordial relation developing among political parties in Uganda at least not in the near future.

Conclusion

Given the illegalities and political dilemma facing NRM transformation and its long established desire for political dominance, at whatever cost it is difficult to see a proper functioning of a multi-party system in Uganda in the near future. However, as Chairman Mao once argued, a journey of a thousand miles begins with one step. We believe that the NRM has been forced to make that single step towards the long match to democracy. It is now up to Ugandans; women, men, youth, civil society and 'everybody', to make sure that this step taken is a right one. And more fundamentally, Ugandans have to struggle for more steps towards a genuine, competitive multi-party system in Uganda. The opposite would mean that all Ugandans, and not only the NRM would be taking a ride on the back of a tiger.

References

Barya , J. J., 2000, *The Making of Uganda's 1995 Constitution: Achieving Consensus by Law?* Kampala: CBR Publications.

Byarugaba, F., 1997, 'The Role of Major Stakeholders in the Transition to Democracy in Uganda', *Makerere Political Science Review Journal,* Vol. 1, No. 1, Department of Political Science and Public Administration, Kampala.

Gingyera-Pinycwa, A. G. G., 1992, *Northern Uganda in National Politics,* Kampala: Fountain Publishers Ltd.

Kulumba, M., 2001, 'Some Reflections on the Social-Political and Economic Reform in Uganda since 1986', Paper presented at the International Summer School of Cross-Cultural Studies, under Polish Commission for UNESCO and Warsaw University Co-sponsorship, Oriental Institute.

Kulumba, M., 2003a, 'The Uganda-Rwanda Intervention in the Democratic Republic of Congo (DRC): A Crisis of Governance in the Region?', *The Egerton Journal,* Kenya: Egerton University Press.

Kulumba, M., 2003b, 'Coalition Politics and Political Stability in East Africa: A comparative study of Uganda National Resistance Movement (NRM) and Kenya National Rainbow Coalition (NARC) experience', Paper presented at the 4th ATWS International Conference 17–19 September.

Mamdani, Mahmood, 1993, *Pluralism and the Right of Association,* Kampala: CBR Publications.

Mugaju, J. and Oloka-Onyango, J., eds., 2000, *No-Party Democracy in Uganda Myths and Realities,* Kampala: Fountain Publishers.

Mujaju, A. B., 1996, 'Political Parties: What they are, how they arise and what they do', Inaugural lecture, Makerere University (unpublished).

Obongo-Aula, Q., 2001, 'From a negotiated Constitution to Elections: The challenges of Democratic Transition under the National Resistance Movement Regime in Uganda', Kampala, Department of Political Science and Political Administration, Makerere University.

Odoki, J. B., 2001, 'The Challenges of Constitution- making and implementation in Uganda', in J. Oloka-Onyango (ed.), *Constitutionalism in Africa,* Kampala: Fountain Publishers.

Oloka-Onyango, J., 1996, 'Commemorating the 1995 Constitution in Uganda: One-step Forward, but how many steps back?' *Uganda Journal,* Vol. 33, Uganda Society, Kampala.

Oloka-Onyango, J. et al., eds., 1996, *Law and the Struggle for Democracy in East Africa,* Nairobi: Claripres.

Sabiiti, Makala, 1996, 'A Review of Yoweri Kaguta Museveni *Sowing the Mastered Seed:* The Struggle for Freedom and Democracy in Uganda', *Uganda Journal,* Vol. 43, Uganda Society, Kampala.

Semogerere and Others vs Attorney General, 2000.

Semogerere and Others vs Attorney General, petition, No. 5, 2002.

Semogerere and Others vs Attorney General, Constitutional Court Ruling, March 2003.

Tambila, K. L., 1996, 'The Transition to Multi-party Democracy in Tanzania: From One State Party to many state parties', in J. Oloka-Onyango et al. (eds.), *Law and the Struggle for Democracy in East Africa*, Nairobi: Claripres.

The 1995 Republican Constitution of Uganda.

The Movement Act, 1997.

The NRM Ten Point Programme.

The Political Parties and Organisation Act (2002).

The Publisher

The **Council for the Development of Social Science Research in Africa** (CODESRIA) is an independent organisation whose principal objectives are facilitating research, promoting research-based publishing and creating multiple forums geared towards the exchange of views and information among African researchers. It challenges the fragmentation of research through the creation of thematic research networks that cut across linguistic and regional boundaries.

CODESRIA publishes a quarterly journal, *Africa Development*, the longest standing Africa-based social science journal; *Afrika Zamani*, a journal of history; the *African Sociological Review*, *African Journal of International Affairs (AJIA)*, *Africa Review of Books* and *Identity, Culture and Politics: An Afro-Asian Dialogue*. It co-publishes the *Journal of Higher Education in Africa* and *Africa Media Review*. Research results and other activities of the institution are disseminated through 'Working Papers', 'Monograph Series', 'CODESRIA Book Series', and the *CODESRIA Bulletin*.

Printed in the United States
46147LVS00002B/402